From the Library of

The Howard's

Shaping Spokane

Jay P. Graves and His Times

A portrait about 1920 of Graves at his desk (*Janice Howe*)

Shaping Spokane

Jay P. Graves and His Times

JOHN FAHEY

University of Washington Press
Seattle and London

Copyright © 1994 by the University of Washington Press
Printed in the United States of America

All rights reserved. No part of this publication may be reproduced or
transmitted in any form or by any means, electronic or mechanical,
including photocopy, recording, or any information storage or retrieval
system, without permission in writing from the publisher.

Library of Congress Cataloging-in-Publication Data
Fahey, John.
  Shaping Spokane : Jay P. Graves and his times / John Fahey.
    p. cm.
  Includes bibliographical references and index.
  ISBN 0-295-97395-1
  1. Graves, Jay P., 1859–1948. 2. Spokane (Wash.)—Biography.
3. Businessmen—Washington (State)—Spokane—Biography.
4. Urbanization—Washington (State)—Spokane—History. I. Title.
F899.S7G684 1994   94-3347
979.7'3704'092—dc20   CIP
[B]

The paper used in this publication meets the minimum requirements of
American National Standard for Information Sciences—Permanence of
Paper for Printed Library Materials, ANSI Z39.48-1984.

Contents

Preface
ix

Chapter 1
Boundary
3

Chapter 2
One of the Boys
22

Chapter 3
Shaping Spokane
35

Chapter 4
The Electric Railway
54

Chapter 5
Granby
74

Chapter 6
Changing Fortunes
88

Notes
103

Bibliography
129

Index
139

Illustrations

MAPS

Spokane and vicinity   45
Spokane & Inland Empire system   64
The Boundary mining district   78

PHOTOGRAPHS

Frontispiece
Jay P. Graves, ca. 1920

Following page 86
Great Northern ore train
Early building at Phoenix
Phoenix in 1909
Great Northern trestle at Deadman's Gulch
Granby smelter under construction
Stephen H. C. Miner and William Yolen Williams
Investors visiting the mines
The Palouse dunes
Crews stringing wire
Crews constructing fill
Rail junction at Spring Valley
Jay Graves and other S&IE officers
Jay Graves and others inspecting S&IE tracks
Tunnel north of Colfax
Nine Mile dam and powerhouse
S&IE Spokane freight terminal

ILLUSTRATIONS

S&IE station at Valleyford
S&IE station at Garfield
Interior of S&IE parlor car
Coeur d'Alene Lake
The "Shoshone Flyer"
S&IE terminal building
Baseball at Recreation Park
S&IE advertisement
William H. Nichols
Hillside cottages at Anyox
Fred B. Grinnell
Granby smelter
Manito Park
Manito Boulevard
Graves's mansion at Waikiki
Sitting room at Waikiki
Front entrance to Waikiki
Modern view of Waikiki
Jay Graves awarded an honorary degree from Whitworth
Jay Graves in his garden
Jay "Pierre" Graves, Alice, and Margaret Bean
Four generations of Graveses
Whitworth College, 1938
The Spokane & Inland Empire's first electric freight locomotive
Holiday travelers at the Spokane terminal
Spokane and Inland Empire electric freight cars
Construction locomotive
Tracklaying on the Coeur d'Alene & Spokane
Train wreck near Coeur d'Alene
Spokane & Inland Empire train
Flatcar going through the Palouse country
Construction train being loaded with gravel

Preface

One of the characteristics of economic evolution in the American West was the entry of pioneer businessmen into fields new to them—farmers turned bankers, clerks become mine managers, and so on. A second characteristic, not confined to the West, was inventing managerial strategies.

The career of Jay P. Graves illustrates both characteristics. In a twenty-year period, Graves, a Spokane hardware merchant and real estate broker, promoted a copper smelter, a suburban railway, and an urban trolley system, and he developed, or made possible the development of, residential areas that determined the shape and direction of Spokane's physical growth.

Graves and other men from roughly 1890 to 1930 stamped Spokane with their vision of the kind of city they thought it ought to be. Trolleys played a role in the real estate expansion of many cities, of course, and speculators made fortunes buying land where the tracks would run next. Jay Graves's trolleys both enlarged Spokane and sold real estate. He enlisted the foremost landscape architects of the time, Olmsted Brothers, to lay out elite districts. For want of a better definition, elite districts are those where the best houses require one or more live-in servants.

One of the challenges in writing about Graves is to make the terrain comprehensible. I have avoided the term "addition," for the most part, in favor of the less precise "district" or "area" and have provided a map. I think you will follow the salient theme, whether familiar with Spokane or not: the effect of street railways on residential expansion.

At the turn of the century, an unknown, brash westerner could hardly hope to get the ears of bankers and investors without the endorsement, real or counterfeit, of prominent men. Graves used the name of the railroad builder James Jerome Hill as his entry.

Graves also skillfully exploited the press. Two newspaper writers, Aubrey L. White, a longtime business associate of Graves's, and Margaret Bean, who admired Graves and became a close friend in his later life, produced articles portraying the man in heroic proportions. They made him a legend in his lifetime.

The following story begins with Graves's promotion of the Boundary, British Columbia, mines and Granby smelter as illustrative of his methods. He left no business or personal papers, as far as I know, so the account has been constructed from the documents and recollections of others and from newspaper and magazine articles.

My final pleasant duty in this preface is to acknowledge those organizations and individuals who rendered me special help. I thank the trustees and staff of the James Jerome Hill Reference Library, St. Paul, who supported my research there and at the Minnesota Historical Society by a fellowship in 1985, and I particularly thank W. Thomas White, curator of the Hill papers, for his attention to my research objectives. Edward W. Nolan, former archivist, Eastern Washington State Historical Society, found materials for me in unexpected places and made useful suggestions; he also listened to my musings on Graves and his activities. Katherine H. Griffin at the Massachusetts Historical Society, Boston, searched unprocessed Adams papers for me; Robert D. Turner, chief, historical collections, British Columbia Provincial Museum, and Brian A. Young, archivist, manuscripts and government records division, Provincial Archives of British Columbia, both in Victoria, went out of their way to find documents and publications I thought useful, and showed an encouraging interest in my inquiries; Charles V. Mutschler, Nancy G. Compau, and David Osterberg, historians of the Spokane area, pointed out new directions and found materials to enhance the telling of Graves's story. My very special thanks to Julidta Tarver, managing editor of the Press, and Carol Zabilski, editor, who steered me ably and graciously from manuscript to print. Many others helped, too, especially archivists and librarians whose contributions, if not names, are acknowledged in the notes. Thank you all. And especially, thanks to my wife, Peggy, whose patience with historical enthusiasms is unwavering.

JOHN FAHEY
Spokane

Shaping Spokane

Jay P. Graves and His Times

CHAPTER 1

Boundary

When this century was very young, no man in Spokane was more admired for his entrepreneurial daring than Jay P. Graves. He took dazzling risks; he consorted with business titans of national repute; he touched with a few thousand dollars enterprises that generated millions; he sprang to grasp opportunities while others hesitated. He was a mining man, a railroad man, a real estate man, and a catalyst for other builders.

Adam Smith must have been thinking of someone like Graves when he wrote that a man "by pursuing his own interest . . . frequently promotes that of society more effectively than when he really intends to promote it." Graves created hundreds of jobs. He advanced Spokane aesthetically and commercially. He brought a college to the city by giving land for a campus. Everywhere in Spokane the stamp of Jay Graves remains.[1]

Thanks to admiring newspaper writers, Graves was eulogized long after he retired from active business. Editors printed retrospective praise for his Spokane estate, Waikiki, his mining and smelting enterprise, Granby Consolidated, his railroad, the Spokane & Inland Empire, implying a question: Why are there no more visionaries like this? Graves achieved legendary stature in his lifetime, and he consciously shaped his legend.

Graves's career mirrors that antipodal mix of acquisitiveness and altruism that puzzles later generations. In person he was slight, of middle height, polite and softspoken to business associates and reporters, a man of light complexion habitually dressed in well-tailored gray so that he seemed colorless and obliging at first meeting. Those who entered the business arena with him found, often belatedly, that he was manipulative, ingenious, and ruthless. He had a frustrating bent for falling ill at crucial moments. Graves formed and discarded friendships as they benefited him. For years, he flaunted the magical name of James J. Hill, the railroad builder, to imply masked power backing him.

It is easy to forget that men of Graves's day invented managerial styles and procedures to operate complex organizations. Graves must have been an astute observer of management practices, especially those of railroads, and respectful of political advantage, although he worked in an era comparatively free of government regulation. His few extant letters do not exhibit the brazen persuasiveness that one would expect.

To understand how Graves operated, it is instructive to examine his first great success, Granby, bigger than anything he had done before, the fountainhead of his legend. Granby lifted him out of the herd of moderately successful businessmen to bell him with singular prominence. He had been a partner in a hardware store and in a real estate brokerage; he once had some small political ambitions. Neither his past nor his substance equipped him to promote a copper company worth millions. The way he went about it set a pattern. Granby is an instructive start toward sifting the legend of Jay P. Graves.

At the turn of the century, the Granby smelter at Grand Forks, British Columbia, was the biggest copper plant in the British Empire, and it was largely Jay Graves's doing.

He drifted into mining somewhat reluctantly because he "was prejudiced against mining; he had seen too many mines fail." But he needed a source of income; Graves's real estate business deflated in the nationwide panic of 1893. Nobody was buying real estate except a few wealthy speculators, undamaged by depression, who were snatching choice bankrupt properties. And Graves's partner was grumpily morose because his wife ran off. Graves seemed unsympathetic, and the partnership soured.[2]

Two dozen or more Spokane bettors had gambled in shares of copper and gold claims near Rossland, British Columbia, and Graves tagged along; he managed the California and Big Three claims for speculators from Montreal. His employers included prominent Canadian politicians: Sir Charles Tupper, the leonine Conservative who served briefly as prime minister, and Rufus H. Pope, a member of the House of Commons. The working superintendent of both claims, a tall, good-natured Welshman, William Yolen Williams, had knocked about western mining for twenty-five years and had scooted from the Coeur d'Alene mines after confronting union anger. Williams would stay with Graves for the next two decades.

Although the California lay idle, it seemed wonderfully promising because the property beside it, the LeRoi, churned out $84,000 worth of copper ore every twenty-four hours (in the estimate of the *Rossland Miner*), enriching its American owners. More Canadian and British investors turned to Rossland, hoping to uncover another LeRoi, and perhaps on the recommendation of his Montreal associates, several hired Graves to oversee their claims. Reluctant he may have been, but as the panic showed signs of lifting, Graves had become a miner.[3]

In the fall of 1895 an old acquaintance, H. P. Palmerston, came to Graves with an offer of shares in copper deposits in the wilderness of the Kettle River drainage west of Rossland. Prospectors had combed the mountains looking for mineral—prospecting always picks up during a depression—and two of them, Henry White and Matthew Hotter, had staked hillside claims they named Old Ironsides and Knob Hill. Of course, a tall tale circulated later about their find: White's packhorse, the story ran, kicked a rock on the trail, which showed copper stains that led to the discovery.[4]

The prospectors gave Palmerston one-fourth of their claims on his promise that he would raise money to explore them, but Palmerston was ailing and, in those times, could not find anyone who would take a chance on that remote splinter of British Columbia. Knowing Palmerston to be reliable, Graves took his shares of the copper claims.

Graves customarily discussed his business with his wife, Amanda, and he surely talked about his new prospects with her and their boarder, Aubrey Lee White, a trim, dandified bachelor of twenty-seven from Maine who clerked in the book department of a pioneer stationer and bookseller, John W. Graham. One imagines these three at supper in the Graves's frame house in snobbish Browne's Addition, talking about mines, and perhaps continuing their descants in the Victorian parlor.

Graves put White to work selling stock in Old Ironsides and Knob Hill at ten cents a share (or less). One of the first buyers was W. A. Ritchie, an architect who, having learned his craft by correspondence, won a competition to design the Spokane County courthouse and, later, the state capitol and other courthouses.

Aubrey White claimed thirty years later that Graves sold his home for money to begin work on Old Ironsides and Knob Hill. In fact, Graves moved his wife and son to the Spokane Hotel, that red brick pile with iron marquee that served as club and residence for mining men. The story current at the time was that he lost his house in a poker game.[5]

Graves incorporated Old Ironsides and hired one of its locators, Henry White, to clear trees and set up a steam-powered hoist and sinking pump to bore an inclined shaft. Then he commenced raising money for development in the classic manner of fortuneless western prospectors: by "making a market" for stock. He took 375,000 of 1,500,000 shares of Knob Hill and 250,000 of 1,000,000 shares of Old Ironsides to sell, confident that the price would soon climb higher than the five or six cents the stock commanded in Spokane. Graves took the precaution of filing on two abutting claims, the Victoria and the Fourth of July, protecting his ground if Old Ironsides turned out, indeed, to be a mine.

To make his pitch sound better, Graves sent a Spokane bank teller and sometime miner, John F. (Frank) Hemenway, to look at Old Ironsides. Hemenway had a local reputation for spotting promising claims. He and Henry White trenched the covering earth to reach an ore body, taking samples for assays, and Hemenway concluded that Graves had a sizable deposit of low-grade copper with small gold and silver values in it. This was no mountain of bonanza copper, no new Butte, but investors reopening Comstock mines in Nevada had recently demonstrated that low-grade ores in large tonnages could be profitable.

As Graves circulated Hemenway's opinion of Old Ironsides, a minor rush of prospectors invaded the forested hills around his claims. New York investors organized the British Columbia Copper Company, Ltd., to work the Mother Lode claim. On a visit to Old Ironsides, Graves saw crews chopping trees and digging on sites scattered across the hills. A mining boom was forming. More men came every day, dragging equipment and supplies seventy miles over rough wagon trails from Marcus (Bossburg), the nearest station on the Spokane Falls & Northern Railroad, struggling uphill most of the way to reach the mountain divide between Boundary Creek and the Kettle River, 4,600 feet above sea level. Here the rounded hills had attracted cattlemen and a few irrigation farmers to grassy western and southern slopes. A hamlet, Grand Prairie, sprouted in the valley, was soon renamed Grand Forks for the forks of the Kettle.[6]

Graves declared that experienced miners told him Old Ironsides and Knob Hill were "the largest surface showings" they had ever seen. Such comments boosted the stock. He predicted that within a year the new camp—now generally called Boundary—would be bigger than Rossland. And perhaps to reassure anyone who thought of Boundary as wild and rugged, he observed that the road from Grand Forks to Greenwood, a new town, was "smooth enough to ride a bicycle over."[7]

Graves needed considerably more capital than stock sales were bringing in. Copper stocks were hard to sell in 1896, even to the penny-stock plungers in Spokane, because Boston speculators upset the market with raiding. But Graves had passing acquaintance with the Montreal men whose mines he managed, and an annual report of the Bank of Montreal convinced him (said Aubrey White) that there must be a lot of rich men in Quebec. Late in 1896 he dispatched White to Montreal to solicit Canadians eager to speculate on western mines. There he could play on Canadian patriotism, on the growing sentiment that Canadians must protect their western provinces from American domination.[8]

White rented a street-level storefront near Victoria Square, filled the window with a display of British Columbia minerals, and lettered "A. L. White & Co." on the door. Soon Graves came along, with his wife and son, to settle in the posh Windsor Hotel, reasoning that a show of prosperity might impress prospective investors.

Graves struck up an acquaintance quickly with Stephen H. C. Miner, a rubber manufacturer who spent his winters at the Windsor and his summers at Granby, Quebec, the site of his factory. At sixty-one, portly, affable, with white sideburns flowing to his ample chin, Miner was "perhaps the foremost businessman of the Eastern Townships," in the opinion of the *Montreal Herald*. (The Eastern Townships are a narrow strip of Quebec where Vermonters migrated after the American Revolution—among them, Stephen's father, Henderson Miner, who prospered as a tanner in the town of Granby.)[9]

Miner was palpably a personage at the Windsor. He and Graves got on well. One pictures them, the earnest, reedy younger man, stylish in gray, moustache neatly trimmed, leaning in his chair toward the grandfatherly listener almost twice his age, attentive, nodding assent occasionally. Within a few days, they realized that they were birds of a feather, putting on colorings of affluence. But if not rich (a business directory estimated his "pecuniary strength" at about $75,000), Miner was on familiar terms with a number of Quebec's wealthy men, particularly stockholders and patrons of the Eastern Townships Bank, of which he was a director.[10]

Miner and Graves soon came together; Miner had the connections Graves needed, the audacity to sell stock in unproven claims, and he could imagine substantial profits for himself in promoting British Columbia copper. The two agreed, however, that they needed substantial testimony on the value of the Boundary mines. Graves hired a mining engineer, "Colonel" Nelson E. Linsley, who headed a mining bureau in Spokane, to inspect and report on his claims.

Linsley found two shallow shafts at Old Ironsides flooded, so he could not go underground, but he liked the mineral showing where the surface earth had been stripped away, and the geology impressed him as favorable for mining. He calculated extensive deposits—he could not guess how large—of low-grade ores distributed more or less uniformly. Linsley's ore samples assayed roughly 1.25 percent copper with by-products of gold and silver. This was "heavy" ore, potentially profitable if processed at or near the mines. Linsley's report contained a felicitous comparison to Alaska's noted Treadwell Mine, often in the news of the day; he thought Old Ironsides's ore higher grade. Because Old Ironsides and Knob Hill ores contained high proportions of silica and lime, they would be virtually self-fluxing, capable of smelting at relatively low cost.[11]

Linsley's evaluation satisfied Miner. He showed it circumspectly to friends in the bank. Graves heard that Miner also inquired discreetly into his and White's reliability. Later, Miner joked with White that the worst anyone said about them was that one was a real estate broker and the other a bookseller without mining experience.

Certainly Miner's colleagues understood the political and economic importance of big mines in Boundary, for Canadian newspapers warned that Americans were gaining control of British Columbia resources and that political annexation to the United States might follow. British and Canadian buyers stripped American stockholders of the best mines at Rossland, not just for profit, but frankly to preserve the district for Canada. A Toronto syndicate took over the War Eagle group, one of Rossland's large producers; an adventurer from London, Whitaker Wright, bought the productive LeRoi and other properties for his British-American Company.[12]

Graves used his time in Montreal, as well, to agitate for railroad lines to Boundary, absolutely necessary to the financial success of the mines. He found the Canadian Pacific Railway's managers lukewarm, unconvinced that Boundary would pay back the cost of building tracks there. To overcome their skepticism, he engaged a mining consultant who periodically served the railroad and soon wrote the CPR vice-president, Thomas G. Shaughnessy, that the consultant "was very favorably impressed" with the claims, adding that entering Boundary would mean "a considerable of tonnage would be furnished your company."[13]

The Boundary mines, British Columbia's demands for rails across the southern half of the province to the coast, and considerable pressure from Victoria and Ottawa to head off another road proposed by D. C. Corbin finally forced the Canadian Pacific to lease (and eventually to buy) the Columbia & Western, a cheaply built narrow-gauge that hauled ores from Rossland's mines to the smelter at Trail. With this purchase, the Canadian Pacific also acquired the smelter, the British Columbia Smelting and Refining Company.[14]

The Canadian Pacific planned to reconstruct the Columbia & Western and extend it east and west—east through Nelson to Lethbridge, and west into Boundary. This would carry the tracks halfway across the province. In return, Ottawa gave the railroad concessions in the Crow's Nest Pass coal district, and both federal and provincial governments granted subsidies.[15]

But the railroad men delayed. The route was mountainous and costly; Corbin's charter application was stalled in committees. For the time being, getting to Boundary continued to be slow and hard. The most direct route lay by the Spokane Falls & Northern from Spokane to Marcus (Bossburg) on the Columbia River, then by stagecoach (or even freight wagon) to Grand Forks, and by wagon or horseback from there to Greenwood. A traveler by this route (Shaughnessy submitted to it once to see the place) left Spokane in the morning and arrived in Greenwood the next afternoon about four o'clock. On the return, the stage for Marcus left Grand Forks at two in the morning.

A resident of Nelson, going to Boundary, of course had to leave Canada for Spokane and re-enter Canada near Boundary. As the crow flies, the distance was about sixty miles; by rail and trail, nearer two hundred. To avoid the trip, Greenwood's citizens joined those of Nelson in paying for a telephone line that allowed them to converse in shouts at $1.35 a minute.[16]

Luck was with Graves. In the middle of 1898, James J. Hill's Great Northern Railway acquired Corbin's Spokane Falls & Northern. With Hill on the scene, Graves (and everyone else clamoring for rails to the interior) had two powerful railroads to play against one another, and Hill's purchase roused the Canadian Pacific. Most important for Graves, the acquisition gave him an occasion for approaching Hill. Hill did not turn him aside, and thereafter for the next decade and a half, Graves would drop Hill's name to imply patronage.[17]

Hill apparently regarded a threat to extend the Spokane Falls & Northern to Boundary and thence to the British Columbia coast as another bargaining chip in his attempts to coerce the Canadian Pacific into surrendering its Soo Line, an American subsidiary that siphoned patronage away from the Great Northern by lower rates in Hill's home territory, Minnesota. Hill began to talk about building to Vancouver. When his crews had entered the Kootenay Lake district of British Columbia in mid-decade, they fought those of the Canadian Pacific, wrecking depots and tracks. If Hill went into Boundary, fireworks could be expected again.[18]

The Canadian Pacific answered Hill with an extraordinary effort. In glacial weather, using horse-drawn scrapers and men with hand tools, it began driving the Columbia & Western to Grand Forks in the winter of 1898–99. The track twisted and curved around the hills, here and there crossing remnants of the Dewdney Trail, cut from coast to interior in the sixties. The first train chugged into Grand Forks on September 18, 1899. By then the CPR was grading a further looping section, north to Eholt and then south through Greenwood to the town of Midway where, said its president, it paused, "a tired horse."[19]

As he earlier had exhorted the Canadian Pacific, Graves now held out to the Great Northern the prospect of a substantial mining and smelting traffic if its tracks came to Boundary. Graves and Miner were assured of rails, Hill or not, and prepared to go into business. They organized three companies, Old Ironsides, Knob Hill, and Granby Consolidated Mining and Smelting Company, Ltd. Granby combined four properties, the Aetna, Victoria, Fourth of July, and Phoenix, clustered around Graves's original claims. Now the two promoters were ready to raise capital by selling stocks in these companies, which newspapers labeled the Miner-Graves syndicate.[20]

Graves traded his interests in his claims for shares of the new companies. Trading what he had, which generally cost him little, for what he wanted would be a technique he used often. Some small investors in the claims were bought out, and a large block of stock in the new companies went to a prominent Montreal securities and insurance broker, Charles E. Gault, apparently the richest of all the early investors in Miner and Graves's companies.[21]

With the prospect of beginning operations, William Yolen Williams came over to Grand Forks from Rossland as manager of Granby Consolidated. He would oversee the mines, located near the top of a hill above Grand Forks, at the end of a steep, winding wagon road cut through the pine forests. On the hilltop a town, Phoenix, was taking shape. Miner and Graves owned most of this ground and consequently would be the town's landlords, principal real estate dealers, and owners of its water system. Phoenix was a workman's town, cut to the pattern of male recreation on the frontier—gambling, slot machines, and more than a dozen saloons. Moralistic citizens would protest Phoenix's base and noisy ways for years before curtailing its "spirited mining days" with laws requiring saloons to provide thirty guest rooms, enforcing Sunday closing, and prohibiting slot machines.

For a time, miners raced horse-drawn sleighs downhill at frightening speeds to Greenwood, terrorizing the residents there, and like as not piling up on the main street. Phoenix would hatch one of the most radical miners' unions in the British Columbia interior. Granby, in Graves style, politely listened to its demands and generally ignored them.

A traveler curious to see Phoenix noted that the first sign of a town was garbage along the roadway. When he walked at dusk he tripped on stones in the streets "till [h]e realized why miners always wear high boots." A few months earlier, he noted, Phoenix had consisted of a small store in a grove of pines. Now it had a mayor, George Rumberger, a prospector who had lived in the area since 1891.[22]

Miner and Graves platted a hillside as Old Ironsides subdivision. Buyers flocked from several hundred miles. "Inside of 24 hours," marveled an editor, "practically every desirable lot was sold for $500 and $600, and within a few days many lots changed hands at a considerable advance." By his estimate, the subdivision brought $100,000, "enough for a first instalment on . . . [a] smelter" that Granby directors proposed to build at Grand Forks. Rumberger placed his own addition to Phoenix on the market and sold all the best lots even before he could file his plat.[23]

With Gault and Miner trading stock in Montreal, Aubrey White moved to a New York office at 30 Broad Street—the building that housed the New York Stock Exchange, across the way from the open-air Curb Market. On the strength of Gault's and Miner's names, the stock rose to 80 cents a share. One small buyer said he had been offered $1.40. More than 450 persons took shares, principally in New York, Montreal, and Philadelphia; a score of Boston men bought in, mostly in the range of 20,000 to 30,000 shares. Sales to Bostonians were encouraging because Boston was, and had been since the Civil War and Michigan copper frenzy, the center for copper investing and trading.[24]

To push sales, Graves and White traveled almost without pause, although White entrenched himself firmly enough in New York to serve on a municipal art committee for parks and boulevards. On his trips from Spokane, Graves often brought his wife and son, Clyde, whom he placed in a New York school.

With funds coming in from stock sales, Graves hired an engineer to design and build a smelter, Abel B. W. Hodges, who had spent ten years with the Guggenheims, America's foremost smelterers, rising from chemist to assistant plant superintendent, and one year as mining consultant to E. H. Harriman, chairman of the Union Pacific Railroad. Shortly before Hodges reached Grand Forks, Thomas Shaughnessy of the Canadian Pacific had written his smelter manager at Trail, Walter Aldridge, asking whether Graves really meant to build a smelter. Aldridge was not keen on the Phoenix mines but answered, "There is little doubt that Graves will go ahead with his smelting scheme." Old Ironsides, thought Aldridge, was probably the best mine, one that would yield enough ore for a "small plant."[25]

The Boundary boom expanded. Within eight miles or so of Greenwood grew a dozen mining camps: Phoenix, Deadwood, Summit, Wellington, and White's Camp, the largest—all with numerous claims. One compelling reason for Boundary's rapid growth was, of course, the Canadian Pacific line, which, as a magazine pointed out, ushered the district to "prominence... impossible previous to the advent of the railroad."[26]

Hodges chose the obvious smelter site north of Grand Forks on the Kettle River, and Graves called for Shaughnessy (who had been elevated to the presidency of the CPR only three weeks earlier) to build a spur to it as quickly as possible. Graves needed to bring in machinery too heavy for wooden wagons. He also buttonholed W. F. Tye, the Columbia & Western construction engineer, with the same exhortation. Tye passed the demand to Shaughnessy: "I presume Mr. Graves has taken this matter up with you, as he would hardly commence the erection of a large smelter without having made some arrangements as to freight on ore, machinery, etc."[27]

If Graves had discussed freight rates with anyone at the Canadian Pacific, it had been in a most casual manner, for Aldridge was still working out a rate schedule for Boundary. Aldridge asked for sample smelter contracts from the Northern Pacific, knowing that American railroads unabashedly juggled rates for traffic concessions and rebates. He also raised the Trail smelter's treatment charges "to get as much general revenue from the Granby... Mines people as possible," believing that if the smelter made enough surplus profit the railroad could afford to cut its freight rate in half to capture Boundary's business against any competitor.[28]

By late fall 1899, the Granby smelter rose on a hillside above Grand Forks. "From the dam across the Kettle river to the superintendent's residence, a distance of fully one mile, there are everywhere gangs of workmen, puffing engines, piles of lumber, loaded teams," the Spokane *Spokesman-Review* reported. A 175-foot earth-filled dam on the river's north fork, "big enough... to take the entire north fork... at low water," and a mile-long wooden flume to the powerhouse were designed by Byron C. Riblet, a young Spokane engineer. (He would become internationally known for tramways and ski lifts.)[29]

While the smelter went up, Canadian Pacific crews laid a two-and-one-half-mile spur to it. Shaughnessy required Granby to pay for the track but, over Aldridge's protest, agreed to refund the cost when production reached 100 tons a day.[30]

Hodges designed a smelter with two double-decked furnaces to process from 150 to 250 tons a day, depending on the mineral content of the ore. Graves was on hand for a muted celebration on April 11, 1900, when the plant ran its first batch—ore from Graves's City of Paris mine south of Phoenix. He had not persuaded the railroad to run a spur there. The ore came by wagon.

Once inaugurated, the smelter ran six days a week. Unlike most companies, Granby observed a Sunday closing law because Miner wished it to; it worked mines and smelter on eight-hour shifts (rather than the customary ten or twelve) in accord with the provincial Mines Regulation Act of 1899. Although the Phoenix miners' union was among the most vocal in British Columbia, Granby seemed to have little difficulty with the men. The local newspaper, the *Pioneer,* remarked that Graves "always had a fashion of running his own business, has never had any trouble with his employees or others. He has paid the best wages, had the best of men. . . . There is no fear of his being involved in labor troubles of any kind." Granby housed single workmen in a three-story brick hotel with electric lights, plastered walls, and steam heat.[31]

Phoenix grew, showing signs of gentility. Homes dotted the hillsides. "By the spring of 1900," said a writer, "the ladies of Phoenix were delicately holding up their skirts as they crossed from boardwalk to boardwalk on dusty Old Ironsides Avenue. Phoenix stage lines . . . made two daily round trips from Greenwood to Phoenix. . . . The cuisine of the Brooklyn Hotel was famous and splendid banquets took place there on occasion."[32]

The whole Boundary country puffed up. London buyers bought the Snowshoe claim, next to the Miner-Graves properties. Canadian buyers invested. Copper, gold, and coal claims were staked along the mountain spine. Robert Wood, who settled on the site of Greenwood, had offered town lots for sale as the railroad approached. In two years his village grew from a few steep trails and tiny post office serving perhaps 200 settlers to a bustling burg of 3,000 with a water system, branches of three Canadian banks, sixteen hotels, fifteen general stores—and soaring ambitions. At a suburb, Anaconda, the Dominion Copper Company built a smelter.[33]

Miner made sure that Grand Forks and Phoenix had a branch and subagency, respectively, of the prestigious Eastern Townships Bank. The bank's directors, determined that the Quebec institution should "break out of its narrow role," moved quickly, once they had been tipped off to Miner and Graves's scheme, in order that they might be first in the field at Boundary.[34]

Men from the Quebec office moved West: Alfred C. Flumerfelt, a bank director, was appointed assistant manager of Granby Con; he represented the bank in British Columbia and Alberta. H. N. Galer, son of a longtime director, was given an office at the Granby smelter.

And not only were mines flourishing. Boundary blossomed with orchards and grain fields, while an incipient lumber business harvested those pines that, a few years earlier, had seemed an inexhaustible nuisance.

The railroad made this possible, of course. But Shaughnessy, a bandbox dandy, fretted over the low returns on the railroad's investment. By one estimate, the Canadian Pacific had spent $7 million building its tracks to Boundary even though mining companies expended no more than $4 million on all of the mining development. And Shaughnessy could see no end to spending, for Jim Hill revealed that he had purchased majority control of the Vancouver, Victoria & Eastern Railway & Navigation Company, Ltd., chartered by the Dominion as an independent line from Vancouver to Midway. The contest was joined for rails from the interior to the coast. Gone was the Canadian road's hope of monopolizing the mining traffic of Boundary.[35]

In the middle of 1901, Shaughnessy received an evasive, even audacious, letter from Hill in response to his inquiry about Hill's intention to lay rail through the Kettle River valley. Hill wrote about the difficulties of building in mountainous north-central Washington. "Allow me to say that we do not wish to invade Canadian territory in any manner beyond what is physically necessary to get access to the country South of the International Boundary," Hill said. "We have no wish to invade the country served by your lines." He went on to remark that he had acted "in a most neighborly manner" toward the Canadian Pacific, even "when you quite drove us out of the business" at Winnipeg. Not a word about his charter to Midway.[36]

The VV&E had long been controversial, a politicians' talisman. Whether its original organizers seriously considered building the line, or whether they aimed all along to profit from selling the charter, remains a question. Even as Shaughnessy read Hill's letter, Great Northern crews were grading to connect the VV&E with the Spokane Falls & Northern, and Hill's surveyors were running preliminary lines from Midway to Grand Forks and Phoenix.

And Hill's men were in the field plotting a line from Montana to the coalfields of Crow's Nest Pass. Shaughnessy soon heard that Robert Wood, from whom the CPR leased land at Greenwood, was dickering to sell some of the same ground to Hill.[37]

A lesser contest threatened for the future mining business of Republic in northeastern Washington, a camp producing more euphoria than mineral. Hill surveyed a branch line there, while Graves, who owned claims, canvassed mineowners to send their ores to the Granby smelter. Montreal men promoted the Republic & Kettle River Railroad from Republic to Grand Forks, and Shaughnessy closed a traffic arrangement with them. When Hill learned of the contract, Walter Aldridge warned Shaughnessy, he "might . . . think you were acting in bad faith with him."[38]

Despite periodic shortages of coke and railcars, the Granby smelter ran more or less continuously, producing copper matte, a crude mixture of sulphides and copper. Granby shipped matte to New York City to be analyzed by one of the industry's foremost samplers, Ledoux and Company, and then sent it to the Brooklyn plant of Nichols Chemical Company for refining into salable copper. A small amount of matte went to Liverpool for refining and sale in Europe.

Thus Graves and Miner had done what the gainsayers said they could not: they had turned Phoenix mines' low-grade ores and Granby's remote smelter into a profitable enterprise and made money in the copper market, which was manipulated by Boston and New York manufacturers and bankers. That market was upset in 1901, a critical time for Granby, by Standard Oil officers' attempt to rig copper prices through a holding company, Amalgamated Copper. For the moment, artificial prices ranging as high as eighteen cents a pound helped Granby to unexpected profits. Graves's feat seemed the stuff of legend.

Albert Ledoux, the New York City copper analyst, came himself to Phoenix to see the mines because rumors spread in New York that Boundary could not last. Mining companies, the gossip ran, were skimming shallow deposits that would soon play out. Ledoux went back to New York to report that "the copper ores of Boundary should . . . profit with copper at 12 cents in New York, and as railway extensions make other ores available . . . the profits should increase." His statement reassured investors. It also helped editors in British Columbia, who reprinted his report whenever the week's news seemed dull.[39]

The provincial minister of mines gave Boundary an even glossier boost. "The general indications are that the ore in this mountain is almost inexhaustible," he wrote, "and it has been demonstrated that the grade of copper improves with depth." The minister counted at least ten producing mines in the Boundary district. The Miner-Graves properties accounted for fully two-thirds of the output, and on the strength of that showing, Granby directors voted to enlarge the smelter.[40]

Graves closed a three-year contract to deliver 700 tons of matte each month to New York refiners and 200 tons to Liverpool. The plan for enlarging the smelter included a converter, a unit to drive air through molten matte to carry off sulphur and leave unrefined copper of higher metallic content called blister. Obviously each ton shipped would be worth more once the converter was in place.

The Canadian Pacific had begun hauling ore down the hill from Phoenix to the smelter in June 1900 and officially opened its branch line in October. Shaughnessy and a party of railroad officials came to Boundary for the occasion. The Phoenix line ended at Old Ironsides, but in November 1901 the CPR ran a spur to Knob Hill. Tortuous hauls by horse-drawn wagon finally ended. The railroad moved forty cars a day, one train loading at the mines, one moving on the track between Phoenix and the smelter, and a third dumping at the smelter. For this, Graves guessed that Granby paid the Canadian Pacific as much as $380,000 a year. Even so, the CPR could not handle all the ore pouring from the mines; dumps of ore towered beside mine portals, waiting shipment. Neither could the smelter work fast enough to process all the ores it received.[41]

Graves and Miner needed to raise new capital to enlarge the smelter. The easiest way, they concluded, was to organize a new company and sell its stock. They merged five companies, including all of those in the Miner-Graves syndicate, into the Granby Consolidated Mining, Smelting and Power Company, Ltd., chartered by the British Columbia legislature on May 11, 1901, with "extraordinary powers." The term "extraordinary powers" is a legalism referring to the broad scope of the company, which was authorized to conduct business as a mining, smelting, real estate, electrical generating and distributing, transportation, and holding company.

This new Granby was licensed to issue $15 million in stock. More than three-fourths of its paper was allocated to shareholders in the old Miner-Graves syndicate. The rest could be sold to raise funds for a larger smelter.[42]

The new Granby also brought in new directors, men connected with the Eastern Townships Bank from which Granby borrowed operating funds. The largest of early stockholders, Charles Gault, dropped out, taking his profits from the higher price that Granby stock now commanded. William H. Robinson, manager of a Quebec branch bank, came on the board, as did Alfred Flumerfelt, who would soon move from Grand Forks to Victoria to expand the bank's investments in the West. There is every indication that Flumerfelt also acted as Miner's spy, keeping him informed about Jay Graves's activities in Boundary.

When they met in Montreal, the stockholders of the new Granby elected Miner president, Graves, vice-president and general manager, and Flumerfelt, assistant general manager. George W. Wooster, distantly related to Graves through marriage, left his post as a teller at a Spokane bank to become treasurer of Granby and liquidator of the syndicate.[43]

Miner's public explanation for consolidating his and Graves's companies was that they operated more efficiently as a unit. Doubtless the merger eliminated some duplication, but he and Graves had tended to manage them as one from the start. Throughout his career, in fact, Graves handled his companies as if they were all of a piece.

The expansion of mining operations and smelter appears to have been immediately financed by a $500,000 loan from the Eastern Townships Bank against which new stock could be pledged. Sales of stock in Granby Consolidated apparently brought in about $800,000. The financing of the new Granby struck some as speculative. Later that year the *Canadian Mining Review* opined that Granby's $15 million capitalization "is enormously in excess of the value of the property," guessing that Miner and Graves had spent no more than $1 million to buy mining claims and build the original smelter.[44]

The *Review* also asserted that Graves and Aubrey White had offered Granby to Amalgamated but had been turned down. Moreover, said the journal, restive stockholders could not learn the estimated value of the company's ore bodies. Miner replied heatedly to the article, but his and Graves's plan from the first had doubtless been to sell the company for a handsome profit. Miner hinted to reporters that he had invested half a million—well beyond his estimated worth—and that Graves was in debt $137,000 to the Exchange National and the Eastern Townships banks for loans on mining properties. In all likelihood, both acquired their mines for modest investments on the promise of developing them.

It was true, moreover, that Miner refused to tell the stockholders how much Granby's ore bodies might be worth; he simply assured them that copper was being mined and sold for a profit. "Instead of striving to pay dividends before your property was fully developed," he explained in a circular to stockholders, the management would "put the properties and plant in a thorough condition to earn and pay dividends regularly." An American periodical, *Engineering and Mining Journal*, printed Miner's views. But the suspicion remained that he and Graves balanced fiscally on thin wire.[45]

Nonetheless, Graves dreamed bigger. The Granby smelter could not handle all of the ores offered it; in fact, as long as it operated, it processed only 4 percent custom or "foreign" ores, that is, the ores from mines other than Granby's. And it supplemented its own power generation by purchasing electricity from West Kootenay Power and Light, which operated Bonnington power station four miles below Nelson on the Kootenay River and sent current sixty-five miles by high voltage wires glistening across the mountains to Grand Forks. To Graves, the need for greater smelting capacity and adequate power seemed an opportunity.[46]

He wrote Thomas Shaughnessy urgently proposing that the Canadian Pacific join him in building another smelter, a custom plant to handle ores of various mines, to stand beside the Granby at Grand Forks. Graves held options on ores from Republic, owned or had options on ten claims in Stevens County, Washington (in the name of the North Western Development Company), and held four claims at Phoenix in his own name and fourteen in Camp White—in all, twenty-eight mines or claims. He offered them all as security for bonds to build a $200,000 smelter and guaranteed that the CPR, if it came in with him, would have all of the traffic from the enlarged Granby as well as his proposed custom smelter, estimating this freight at worth $800,000 a year. Shaughnessy should act confidentially and speedily, Graves urged, because "various shareholders have to be dealt with" in his properties.[47]

Shaughnessy must have been tempted; he could cut Hill off from nearly all of Boundary's mining traffic by joining Graves. But Aldridge continually warned that Boundary's mines were overrated, and Ledoux in New York advised caution. Shaughnessy concluded that a custom smelter would be "impractical" for the CPR and turned Graves down.

If Shaughnessy would not join him, perhaps Hill would. Graves discovered that some large stockholders in Granby Consolidated, Miner among them, were ready to take profit and run. He went secretly to Jim Hill asking a loan of $2 million to buy 500,000 shares of Granby at an average of $4. Added to the 150,000 shares he and two employees owned, Graves told Hill, this would be enough stock to "absolutely have control in our own vault."[48]

When he outlined his scheme to seize Granby, Graves was on his way to New York with a stopover in Montreal. He reviewed his plan in a four-page letter to Hill, ending, "Of course without your road into our smelter at Grand Forks or our mines at Phoenix you could not consider this. . . . I trust until that time arrives, viz, the completion of your lines, that positive secresy will be maintained. . . . It will require secresy to enable me to secure the amount of stock suggested." Jim Hill could read between the lines as well as anyone. If Graves grabbed Granby with Hill's help, the Great Northern would monopolize the mining traffic of Boundary. He agreed to advance $25,000 (on the security of Graves's stock) for a down payment toward 500,000 shares, and Graves went on to Montreal, wiring Hill for instructions for picking up the money.[49]

But Graves's scheme unraveled in Montreal. Hill had not sent the $25,000, and Graves could not deal without this earnest money. He was embarrassed, he later told Hill. Miner indeed was selling. William H. Nichols of Nichols Chemical, the New York refiner that processed much of Granby's blister, placed a call on 225,000 shares, almost half the stock Graves hoped to snare. Miner and his friends delivered 100,000 shares to Nichols and took an additional 125,000 from Granby's treasury, and—not suspecting Graves's bid against them—invited him to join in the sale. He swallowed hard and went along.

Now, only if Nichols reneged could Graves hope to grasp control of the company. He apologized to Hill for his frantic calls for money. "Without doubt my action at Montreal was hasty, but I was dealing with persons that I felt haste was a necessity. Mr. Nichols . . .

was in the humor to buy into Granby." Hill sent Graves $25,000 in New York in case Nichols changed his mind, but the chance had passed. Nichols bought the stock and, in the next few months, brought wealthy friends from the copper industry into Granby Consolidated.[50]

Even though his plot for preempting Granby had misfired, Graves benefited impressively from his adventure in Boundary. Now he associated with leading figures in the copper industry, for he remained vice-president and general manager under Nichols. He had gained a sympathetic backer in James J. Hill. He had tested his skills as manager of a complex corporation. He had pumped up a modest risk to million-dollar proportions by pyramiding companies. And he had captivated Spokane, lifted himself above the crowd in his adopted hometown, and had launched the legend—the man of daring who prevailed against daunting odds.

CHAPTER 2

One of the Boys

Jay Graves said that he arrived in Spokane on Christmas Eve 1887. A newspaper, the *Spokane Falls Review,* mentioned a proposed street railway that day, a "motor road" from the north to the south city limits. Maybe that was an omen.

Christmas Eve fell on Saturday. The harmonies of a church school cantata at the opera house drifted to throngs in the frozen streets stepping around snowdrifts, piles of lumber, and trenches for gas and water lines lighted by flickering store windows. Sidewalk barkers touted raffles in their stores, gay with wreaths and ribbons. The holiday quickened the vaulting spirits of a growing town.

Business had been slow in the first years of the eighties, but with arrival of the Northern Pacific Railroad's main line in 1883, recapture of the county seat in 1886, and a million-dollar yield from the Coeur d'Alene mines, Spokane Falls now throbbed with "strange faces," observed the *Review.* "Every train contributes its quot[a] to the growing population." The editor marveled at a construction boom—"so many foundations it would keep an army of reporters busy trying to keep run of them." With thirty-eight fire hydrants, twenty arc lights "at principal crossings," fifty-two telephone boxes, and a nightly variety show, Spokane Falls would—if it could uniform its policemen, run streetcars on schedule, and turn on the gas—"have symptoms of a metropolis."[1]

Graves had been prepared for the town's buoyancy by his older brother, Frank, a bear of a man with a rumbling voice, who had come in 1884 after practicing law in Carthage, Illinois. Frank rented an office for fifteen dollars a month and carried wood upstairs for the round stove that heated it. He plunged quickly into real estate speculation. This Graves would luminesce in the courts for nearly sixty years, a showman of robust opinion, wayfaring in politics and real estate; he was a cynosure from the moment he first disembarked at the railroad station, delighting gawkers by wearing a silk hat and cutaway coat as he stepped off majestically into Spokane Falls's muddy lanes.[2]

Frank was the eldest of four sons of John J. Graves and his second wife, Orilla Berry. In 1839, when John had been 20, his father, Reuben Graves, moved his family from Kentucky—to get out of a slave state, it was said—to newly opened farmland on Round Prairie in western Illinois, settling by the hamlet of St. Mary's, near Plymouth, a village on the state road that led past the Hancock County seat, Carthage, to the Mississippi River.

Reuben was among the original members of the St. Mary's Baptist church and later joined the founders of a Methodist Episcopal church at Plymouth in a time when traditional churches were regarded as bastions against the Mormons headquartered at Nauvoo, barely thirty miles distant.

Frank was born at St. Mary's in 1857; Jay, named for his great-grandfather, on June 27, 1859; Carroll, in 1861; and William, in 1866. The boys worked on the farm and attended local schools. Perhaps they showed little inclination to be farmers or there was no place for them, for Frank and Jay graduated from college at Carthage, about fifteen miles northwest of Plymouth. Established by Lutherans in 1870, Carthage College offered studies in languages, English, mathematics, music, and the natural sciences, and enrolled about 100, many training to be elementary school teachers.[3]

After reading law, Frank opened his practice at the county seat, married Esta Maud Ferris, daughter of a nearby farmer, and labored as a trial lawyer. Jay went into the hardware business at Plymouth, indulged in town politics, and on October 9, 1880, married Amanda Cox, whose father had come from Virginia to farm about ten miles from the Graves's homestead. Both Carroll and William followed their oldest brother into law.

Western Illinois settled into prosaic routine, however, while tales of adventure and prosperity drifted from the West in letters and newspaper accounts. Frank, Maud, and their infant son set out for Spokane Falls with an offer of a partnership from an attorney. They arrived, Frank said, on Christmas Day 1884. As Spokane Falls's fortunes improved, he urged his brothers to come. And they did, one after the other. Late in December 1887, Jay, Amanda, and their five-year-old son, Clyde, left Plymouth to move west. In later years,

Illinois neighbors recalled that Jay pleaded poor health as his reason for moving; it was to be a familiar apology, for he was not robust.

Frank introduced his brother to business acquaintances, and shortly Jay joined an agreeable, dogged little man with a beak nose, Charles F. Clough, a stationer and bookseller who switched to real estate as a more promising line. "Real estate is changing hands rapidly," declared the *Review,* "despite the cold weather." Clough and Graves closed their first deal together on January 14, 1888, buying parts of two lots east of the business district.[4]

The Spokane Falls of 1888 was an inelegant town of perhaps 4,000 poised for explosive growth, laid out in a grid. The buildings were mostly frame structures on thirty or so blocks along dirt streets, between the river and the Northern Pacific tracks; homes in piney groves mixed with commercial structures, many thrown up in haste with green lumber and never painted. Immigrants poured through, looking for farms in the countryside or places in town. Spokane Falls offered them a barn as overnight shelter. As the demand for lots inflated prices, the *Spokane Times* clucked that "the heavy property owner and the real-estate agent are the only parties benefited," while the *Review* crowed that "the rapidity of growth is simply marvelous."[5]

Marvelous, indeed. By the census of 1890, the town would bloat to nearly 20,000 (and a decade later, to 36,000), expand in area from two square miles to more than twenty, and add political districts or wards as it grew. Like many another in the West, the city government—an unpaid mayor and common council elected from the wards, inexperienced, partisan, and nearly overwhelmed by breakneck expansion—struggled to provide the barest municipal services (with a seven-mill property assessment): to fund police and fire protection, domestic water, sewers, and streets and to regulate utilities and thirty-four miles of street railways franchised to private owners. For its efforts, the council would be scolded by the newspapers: "Mud on Riverside . . . deep enough to drown a yearling calf."[6]

Business mushroomed in an uproar with openings and closings almost overnight, men leaping from one field to another, bankers betting depositors' funds on mines, projected railroads, timber, and mills—and everyone trading in land. Jay Graves served briefly as a director of an insubstantial board of trade, but it could not unite the business community and reorganized in 1891 as a chamber of commerce. Graves's partner took a turn as mayor.

With growth, Spokane Falls flaunted pretensions: it was going to be a great city because a few men resolved to make it so. Two early settlers, Anthony M. Cannon and John J. Browne, had bought half of the townsite from the founder, James N. Glover, and set out to sell it. Before 1890 Cannon and Browne had drawn around them the doers, the builders, the men who took charge. Jay Graves joined them; he was popular, with a gift of mimicry and a knack for storytelling; his name would be linked with a number of endeavors to publicize or enlarge the town.

Glover, Cannon, and Browne opened banks; Cannon and Browne promoted the Auditorium, a building for offices and a theater with a stage larger than any other in America. They and their ilk, a self-annointed gentry, put up buildings, played mayor, dealt in finance and real estate, and guided the citizenry as a cabinet of "progressive" men, arbiters of conduct and dress for the town. They regarded as their due the privileges and perquisites of city leaders. In this spirit, Cannon bequeathed money for a statue the citizens might wish to raise in his memory.

The ethics of business then, however, implied wariness. The *Review* might say that "moral progress must be co-ordinated with material progress. The one cannot exist when the other is absent," but businessmen set the standards of business morality. They admired the adroit bargainer in politics and in business. The *Review* condoned a little cupidity with its editorial view that "men are but older boys, playing another game than marbles . . . the actual game of production." And boys would be boys. Gambling was common in Spokane Falls at every social level. Homes and real estate changed hands at pool or poker. A man with money had his chances to make a killing.

A mile west of the business district, Cannon and Browne platted abutting additions (with Spokane Falls's first park) and laid a four-and-one-half-mile horse-trolley line to carry residents between home and office. Theirs became an elite residential district. By no means unique to Spokane, the inducements of a streetcar and a park offered a lesson in real estate merchandising that was not lost on Jay Graves and other men promoting new additions. Graves himself took a house in Browne's.[7]

Spokane Falls, however, lacked capital to match its ambitions.

Encouraged by Cannon and his cronies, a traveling Hollander, Herman A. Van Valkenberg, organized the Northwestern and Pacific Hypotheekbank, funded by bonds sold mostly in Amsterdam and Rotterdam, raising more than $2 million to lend in Spokane Falls. Cannon was among the mortgage bank's incorporators and one of its principal borrowers.[8]

The Dutch lender had not been in business long before Spokane Falls burned—two dozen blocks, most of the business houses, consumed on August 4, 1889. The town's cocky businessmen determined to rebuild, and they borrowed from the accommodating Dutch to erect massive, fire-resistant structures of brick and granite along Riverside Avenue and the intersecting streets of the central district. "I have never seen a small town . . . which offers such an overwhelming impression of monumental buildings," one Hollander wrote to Amsterdam, noting that many builders "over-reached themselves to force its development when they should have been more cautious and allowed natural growth to occur."[9]

Active in real estate trading before and after the fire, Clough and Graves dealt in commercial and residential property, concentrating west of the central business district where Graves, in his own name, also acquired lots in Cannon's Addition. On several occasions, he bought from Clough. The partners added investment brokering to their line. For weeks after the fire, Clough and Graves shared a tent on Riverside Avenue with Cannon's Bank of Spokane Falls, while blackened debris still cluttered streets.[10]

Spokane Falls not only rebuilt but mounted an Industrial Exposition in 1890 to demonstrate its revival and claim its central place in the interior Northwest. F. Lewis Clark, the wiry, caustic son of a wealthy Maine banker, served as president; Jay Graves, on the executive committee (although his preferred site was rejected). In a colorful gazette published for the exposition, Graves was among those who bought space for a portrait and biographical sketch in a section titled "Representative Men."

About the same time, the Washington legislature sent a commission to choose the site for a state agricultural college. Graves was one of the men who escorted the commissioners to alternative 360-acre tracts that Spokane Falls proffered for the school. Eventually, however, the college settled in Pullman.[11]

To attract prospective buyers of real estate, Clough and Graves sponsored a handsome booklet, *The City of Spokane,* by John R.

Reavis, secretary of the chamber of commerce, with photographs of main streets and buildings. (Spokane dropped "Falls" from its name in 1891.) With slight exaggeration, the booklet bragged of major structures and their costs: Hotel Spokane, $240,000; Auditorium, $300,000; Exposition, $100,000; Lindelle Block, $115,000, and so on. It declared that Spokane, with no railroad in 1880, now was the hub for seven. The seventh, the Great Northern, was on its way; its first passenger train would arrive on May 28, 1892, puffing over the right-of-way that its president, James J. Hill, had bullied out of the city.[12]

Clough and Graves, investing in the west end, built six two-story houses of six rooms each on west Riverside for resale and a few months later contracted with Cannon to sell his addition "on very easy terms to those intending to build good residences," as their advertisement read. With the construction of a ward school (later the Washington) the addition attracted families. Clough and Graves also handled the Union Pacific Addition, west of Browne's, promoting it for factory sites; and to the east, the firm offered twenty-eight residential lots in Ross Park on the river's north bank at the end of a new electric street railway.[13]

Carlines, like those to Cannon's and the Ross Park additions, sold housing away from the center of town. In those times, home buyers came largely from professional and merchant classes; unskilled workmen and artisans rented. Buying a home required cash or a substantial down payment, perhaps one-third of the price, with a short-term mortgage, rarely more than a year or two, often with a final balloon payment. As families vacated homes for newer or bigger ones, however, less affluent people bought their old ones—"buying up," they called this—causing a rippling outward migration from downtown that eventually ringed the business area with older housing left by those who could afford to move out where the streetcars took them.[14]

In the years after the big fire, Spokane's residential districts crept across the flatlands north of the river and up the nearest southern hills. Commercial construction slowed by 1891, but housing expanded, the choice of sites decreed largely by developers who laid out the plats, installed water mains, and drew oblong grids of streets and alleys.

The best-selling districts by the early nineties were those with street railway service, and the railways were often built by the men who platted and offered the homesites. The City Park Transit through Heath's Addition to Lidgerwood Park, for example, was organized by David and Chester Glass, who, with Patrick Byrne, acted as agents for the Lidgerwood Addition; the Ross Park line; and the Spokane & Montrose Motor Railway (originally propelled by steam), by Francis H. Cook, looped up the southern slopes to Grand Boulevard and the undeveloped tangle that Cook called Montrose Park.[15]

Clough and Graves did not plat an addition, but the partners were busy representing men who did. In a welter of real estate agencies, theirs seemed lively and stable, although they moved offices frequently. To their real estate and investment activities, they added title insurance, forming the Washington Abstract & Title Guaranty Company, a concern they housed in the basement of a one-story marble bank, an architectural gem in Corinthian style that Cannon built in 1892 at the northwest corner of Riverside and Mill (Wall). Graves was president of the new company for six years until he and Clough leased it to the owner of the Spokane Abstract Company.

In 1892, Graves ran for mayor, nominated on the sixth ballot of a contentious convention of city Republicans. The *Review* called him "one of the best knwon businessmen in the city" and hailed him as "very near . . . an ideal candidate for mayor . . . a man of family and property interests . . . with correct business and training methods." Graves modestly pledged a "safe, business-like, conservative administration," which, given the city's financial straits, was more than any politician could deliver. He lost 1,674 to 1,414, to Daniel M. Drumheller. The *Review* blamed his defeat on a "bogus interview" in the Democratic *Spokane Chronicle* and on "downright treachery of certain disaffected elements," labeling the election a "show of petty, miserable rivalry among politicians."[16]

After his defeat, however, Graves was not wholly outside the political game. When Spokane County commissioners revealed that they would call for bids on a bridge across the river at Cedar instead of one at Post, the *Spokesman* of Spokane charged that Clough and Graves, who had joined the secret deliberations, were "pushing" the bridge because they "have large property interests in the west end of the city." The newspaper sneered that the proposed Cedar span would be "a $250,000 boodle bridge." More than 300 persons had petitioned for it—Graves's name was first among the signers.

James Glover stalled the plan by injunction, and depression soon killed it.[17]

The panic of 1893 leaped snarling upon the country late in the spring. The New York stock market crashed on May 5. Distress rolled across America; it would be the worst depression between the 1870s and 1929 and compound the torment of Spokane's rebuilders, land speculators, farmers in debt, and merchants who depended on their business. All were caught with heavy obligations in an unforgiving economy.

The panic swept aside a legion of ruling pioneers in Spokane. Cannon's bank failed in June, followed within weeks by Browne's, Glover's, and four others, seven of ten in the city. The Hypotheekbank and other lenders, fearful for their own safety, foreclosed aggressively, taking the lands and buildings pledged as security for loans. The pioneer men who had founded, promoted, and steered Spokane were bankrupt. Cannon died on a futile mission to recoup.[18]

The panic did not destroy everyone, did not maul uniformly. While hundreds lost fortunes and property, a man with money could select among unique bargains in real estate. For example, John A. Finch, miner-turned-real-estate speculator, foreclosed Muzzy's Addition; the Hypotheekbank took Cannon's and Cook's additions, and the Provident Trust, Cook's street railway. Sales of abandoned, foreclosed, and tax-delinquent property in and near Spokane would go on for years. The brothers Frank and Will Graves, law partners, bought business sites, and Frank, some choice undeveloped residential lots as well as Glover's mansion on the south hill. Jay Graves took land near the Little Spokane River, north of the city.[19]

Thus, distress for many meant opportunity for a few. While jobless men occupied the old city haymarket, intending to march with Coxey, by contrast 73 borrowers repaid the Hypotheekbank. A newspaper estimated that there were 650 homeless persons in Spokane, sleeping in saloons or a tabernacle. On the other hand, contractors built a flour mill and 400 new houses (average cost $1,000) in the city during 1894. The state underwrote an insane asylum at nearby Medical Lake and a normal school at Cheney and Spokane County built a French Renaissance courthouse as relief projects. But when the City of Spokane called on individual citizens and businesses to be sureties for a new waterworks, 155 pledged from $500 to $40,000. Neither Graves nor Clough, incidentally, signed as surety.[20]

Although they would continue their business partnership for three more years, Graves and Clough began taking separate paths. Graves was drawing closer to Lewis Clark, who had come to Spokane Falls in 1885 and had since ridden his horse all around the town to deduce the likely direction of future expansion. He and his father, Jonathan Clark, bought vacant land northeast and east of Glover's original townsite to hold for resale. Now, with hardship forcing sales, they snapped up choice sites. Clark emerged from the panic as a power in Spokane's real estate market.

Clark's money, his aptness for exploiting real estate, and his new interest in mines attracted Graves. Opposites in temperament— Clark was taciturn and Graves outgoing—they shared the conviction that money could be harvested from informed speculation in real estate and mining stocks. A number of Spokane men, including Frank Graves, had taken flings in the penny stocks of gold and copper mines near Rossland and the lead and silver claims of the Coeur d'Alene district. A lucky few would realize thousands for their pennies, sidestep bankruptcy, and buy bargain properties in Spokane.

As receiver of the First National Bank, Clark held high hopes for the bank's largest asset, the Last Chance Mine in the Coeur d'Alenes, not so much for its ore bodies as for its strategic location near the Bunker Hill and Sullivan properties, the acknowledged prize of the district. He and others, including Fred B. Grinnell, real estate broker and receiver of the Spokane Savings Bank (associated with First National), formed a stockholders pool that eventually gave Clark control of the Last Chance with Charles Sweeny, its promoter and manager. Both Clark and Grinnell, incidentally, were developing additions near the site of the Great Northern Railway shops at Hillyard, a suburb northeast of Spokane.[21]

Graves lent Lewis Clark his support in a face-off with the city council over a new source of domestic water for the city. With customary foresight, Clark and his father had bought a quarter section on the Spokane River from the Northern Pacific. This eventually proved to be a key property for a proposed upriver pumping plant and wells for water. If the Clarks paid the railroad's going rate of $2.50 an acre for unimproved land, they conceivably got the site for $400. In 1892, the younger Clark offered the city his land and water rights for $80,000. Water was both an urgent necessity and a political issue. The *Review* snapped that the "Clark gang" would "delay a solution" to the water problem (although membership in the alleged gang was never clarified), while Mayor Drumheller demanded a competent engineer to design a system, observing that he had already seen the source "permanently" located more than once. In a special election, Clark's site fell short of the three-fifths majority of votes needed. But a year later, when tempers had cooled, the city acquired the property on his terms.[22]

Throughout the water struggle, Graves had done what he could to advance Clark's position. Graves's own situation was quite different; he was suing two delinquent debtors for $5,000 cash and $10,000 in mortgages due him on property he acquired as their agent. Perhaps a shortage of funds from this transaction pushed the Graveses temporarily out of their house, mortgaged to the Hypotheekbank for $8,000; they moved in with the family of Hanford W. Fairweather, vice-president of Glover's failed bank. Fairweather, Glover, and others had organized a new company, the Union Trust, to deal in trust management, hoping to make a comeback.[23]

It must have been Clark's money that enabled Graves to bid for city warrants for a new water system. Graves offered to buy $150,000 in warrants, stipulating that the city set aside 60 percent of its future water revenues to retire the debt. The Spokane brokers Charles Theis and Henry C. Barroll, representing an eastern buyer, offered to take the new and older outstanding warrants up to $300,000; their bid required 8 percent interest and diversion of 75 percent of water revenues to retire the paper. Theis and Barroll had cannily joined the contractor, who was to pay the commission on their warrants. Their contract precluded a competing offer. The council could only ask Graves to withdraw for "a small commission."[24]

Graves also speculated in mining; he invested in a small way in Idaho and Canadian prospects and agreed to manage several properties at Rossland for absentee owners. Clough, on the other hand, preoccupied himself with a campaign for city charter revision. The partners separated on friendly terms; Graves formed a real estate, investment, and mining brokerage in the basement of the marble bank building on Riverside.

The panic was waning in 1896, immigration starting up again, and business reviving. "Vacant stores and dwellings have found tenants, and $800,000 has been expended on new buildings," the *Spokesman-Review* of Spokane said in its reprise of the year. "The jobbing trade has increased 42 percent, and the retail trade has grown 30 percent." Although the Coeur d'Alene mines often shut under threat of labor violence, Corbin's Spokane Falls and Northern Railroad to Rossland "added another stroke to the wheel of prosperity that is revolving so rapidly to Spokane's renown. It has made Spokane the virtual headquarters of Rossland's mining men, and the acknowledged trade center of the entire Trail Creek region."[25]

The Northwest was entering a boom that would last until after 1910. In Spokane, residential lots that sold in 1887 for $700 now brought $1,000. An appraiser for the Hypotheekbank reported to his home office that "rents are considerably higher; there is a demand for rental homes; some good homes are being built; indeed, there are many signs of returning confidence" in the city. But setting market values on the bank's foreclosed real estate must wait, he went on, "until new capital comes to Spokane or the buying power of the present population improves," and the Dutch would need several years to sell off holdings acquired since the crash of 1893.[26]

The conditions created a bonanza buyer's market in real estate. Some outside capital was at work: the Provident Trust (Boston) and the Pennsylvania Mortgage Company snapped up Spokane property, and George C. Adams, a great-grandson of the sixth president of the United States, snared large tracts for the Adams Real Estate Trust at sheriff's auctions. George's uncles, Charles F. Adams II and Brooks Adams, also nabbed Spokane land.[27]

Much of the buying in 1896 and for a decade after, however, fell to a select cluster of Spokane men with money—among them, William H. Cowles, John A. Finch, Frank P. Hogan, Frank H. Graves, D. C. Corbin, and the redoubtable short-lived partners Lewis Clark and Charlie Sweeny—who tucked away the sites of a future Davenport Hotel, Spokane Club, federal building, Empire State Building, and other prime locations.[28]

These men were not the sole buyers, of course, for buying was widespread as times improved, but they were the ones who would play commanding roles in shaping Spokane—men positioned by fortune to step in when the older generation of leaders, Cannon's clique, lost their places. The new men of property avoided public office and to a degree ignored public opinion; to them, civic progress meant profitable development of their holdings. By and large these men had come to Spokane with the purpose of prospering with a growing town.

Throughout the city's transformation for the next twenty years, they would decree the physical pattern and locations of business and residential districts, parks, and street railways and, by prestige and example, dictate political and social standing. Cowles gave them their voice: he arrived in 1891, aged twenty-five, with an interest in the *Spokesman;* bought the *Review* in 1893, and published the first *Spokesman-Review* on June 29, 1894; in 1897, he acquired the evening paper, the *Chronicle.*

Regardless of their backgrounds, these men agreed on the kind of city Spokane ought to be. They conceded that business prominence implied obligations to the community. One responsibility of businessmen in the nineties was to fashion a city that was beautiful as well as utilitarian. The City Beautiful movement had gathered momentum for half a century; it was largely crystallized in the grand vision of the 1893 World's Columbian Exposition in Chicago.

Business interests in many cities rallied to the cause of municipal elegance that took the form of artistic public buildings, monuments, parks, vistas, treed avenues, and other amenities. In their view, urban progress could be managed, physically and politically, to create a city matched to their vision. The mechanisms they used to achieve their goals were park boards and park systems, new forms of city government, planning councils, and on occasion, simple power.[29]

For the residential real estate developer, the City Beautiful idea offered tangible benefits. Parks separated commercial from residential districts, raising values. Parks created traffic patterns that influenced land prices. Parks made natural fire barriers and vistas to attract home buyers. And choice homesites could be manufactured with trees, ponds, gardens, and grass.

New notions of civic management emerged. As early as 1897, the *Spokesman-Review* pointed out that "conditions may never again be so favorable for acquiring park land," opining that parks ought to be donated by landowners. Although there was little immediate response, the seed was sown. In a relatively short period, the select businessmen of Spokane, like those of many cities, advocated charter reform for better government, a park system, and eventually a plan commission. Most of the large land buyers of 1896 eventually gave land for parks, enlisting the preeminent landscape designers of the nation to lay them out. In this shaping of the city, Jay Graves would play a central role.[30]

CHAPTER 3

Shaping Spokane

Jay Graves plucked the Montrose streetcar company as a business for his son, Clyde, in November 1902. The Montrose, three and one-eighth miles of track and four cars, was originally built by Francis Cook to promote his extensive real estate holdings on the southeast heights overlooking the city of Spokane. Cook's land came with the streetcar company. At the summit of Cook's hill, as the locals called the ground, Cook set aside Montrose Park. But he lost the streetcar company in the panic of 1893. When Graves took over, the future park was a wooded tangle of underbrush and basaltic rockpiles as big as houses.

Cook powered his little line with steam, at first, but by 1902 the Montrose had been converted to electricity. Cook had never sold enough homesites to use all the track he laid. The cars started at Washington and Riverside, in the heart of the city, climbed Washington southward to Cook's ornamental home on the lip of his hill, and turned around, although the track ran another mile or two farther south. One problem was water service. Cook got his household water from a spring, but the lots beyond had none.

The Montrose had been financed by a loan from the Spokane office of Provident Loan and Trust. When Cook's businesses failed, Provident tried to find someone who would take over the line. Finally a Minneapolis investment company bid $52,500 for it, intending to use the Montrose to promote real estate sales to eastern buyers. And when the Minneapolis firm backed out, Provident gratefully turned the company over to Jay Graves. It was a bargain, and in his customary style, Graves set out to make an investment of almost nothing into an enterprise worth millions.[1]

The panic over, Spokane was growing rapidly north, south, and east of the central core. Houses sold quickly. Speculators and newcomers bought land, sometimes unseen, at runaway prices. Speculative development of real estate was a game that Graves understood very well. He plunged in.

Reorganized as the Spokane Traction Company on February 1,

1903, Graves's new streetcar line in May received a liberal franchise from the city allowing him to build anywhere he pleased. The franchise, to a large degree, demonstrated the city council's discontent with the Washington Water Power Company, which had purchased and consolidated all of the other streetcar routes. Graves's twenty-five-year franchise waived compensation to the city until January 1908 and permitted the Coeur d'Alene & Spokane, a suburban electric railroad, to enter Spokane on Traction Company tracks to a terminal at First and Washington; it authorized Graves to lay rails immediately north and south on Washington and to extend eastward along Boone Avenue to the city limits and on Second Avenue to Sherman Street. These routes would reach the developing areas of the city. Some grumbling about freight trains on city streets quieted after Graves explained that the company would carry freight in cars that looked like passenger cars.[2]

Graves floated $366,000 in bonds for expansion. With this money and his franchise, he would not hesitate to run a line wherever he found business, even when his route ran into places already served by Washington Water Power carlines. He was confident, indeed, that invading WWP routes was what the city council wanted him to do.

"It has always been a mystery why the Washington Water Power allowed the Traction Company to get a foothold in Spokane," the *Spokesman-Review*'s editor would muse some years later. "It could have bought for a song the nucleus around which the Traction Company system was built." There had been "rising popular sentiment" for another transit service, the editor concluded. The power company was out of favor, another editorial declared; its local officials "have shown a disposition to euchre the city . . . and hold a club of litigation" over it. The newspaper was incensed at the power company's shuffling of unused franchises for political and financial advantage.[3]

Real estate developers were cramped, in a time of growth, by WWP's refusal to serve new additions. "Our policy of not extending lines is centralizing home building and increasing patronage on lines already constructed," the company observed in its 1901 annual report. With Graves's entry into the street railway business, however, the power company foresaw "a return to . . . speculation that marked the period before the panic of 1893," with new carlines fueling speculation.[4]

WWP also reported that it expected new street railways to be "customers for a considerable amount of power." It was right about that. Although Graves would eventually build his own power system, he bought current from Washington Water Power throughout the life of his street and interurban roads.

Graves's enlargement of the Montrose offered real estate developers the happy opportunity to play one railway company against the other, soon forcing WWP also to extend lines into new areas. Except for Browne's Addition and a few houses along the river, Spokane's bluffs and hills, river views, and valley vistas remained to be platted, and nearly all of them, foreclosed in 1893, had been snatched up in the sell-off after 1896 by investors who held them for development as superior residential sites. They were large areas of piney flatlands and weedy hillsides. Carlines could improve even these homely locales, parks enhance them, landscaping transform them, and buyers would pay higher prices than for lots in standard grid plats.

In many ways the Spokane of 1900 mirrored the ostentation of industrial urban America. As the town flourished, merchants, mining and lumber magnates, bankers, lawyers, doctors, and others— even a handful of manufacturers—not only could afford expensive housing but demanded striking homes to testify to their preeminence in society and business.

They met in exclusive clubs—the Spokane, the University, and the Country; they directed businesses and banks, patronized theaters, summered at Coeur d'Alene, Liberty, and Hayden lakes, rode in chauffeured automobiles, and relished recognition by common people. On Sundays, their pastors assured them that God blessed their superior thrift and industry.

The publisher of a 1902 Blue Book of Spokane society printed a calling-day and address list of 388, which, he confidently asserted, "contains a majority of those people who are entitled to the claim and recognition of 'Society.'" The three Graves brothers, Jay, Frank, and Will, made the Blue Book.[5]

To develop the real estate along Cook's Montrose line, Graves organized the Spokane-Washington Improvement Company with wide powers to lay out additions to Spokane, install water systems, grade streets, establish and maintain parks, and so on. The new company would plat as homesites a large district on the south hill, roughly from Fourteenth Avenue to Thirty-seventh between Division and Hatch streets. It was all rough, overgrown, and studded with basaltic outcrops.

South of Thirty-seventh near Grand, Graves sold fifty acres to the Spokane Country Club for $17,000, expecting that the planned clubhouse and nine-hole golf links would attract buyers to sites he would offer surrounding the course. (The club later sold after its clubhouse burned.) A section south of Thirty-third and west of the links was platted as Acre Tracts, where buyers might tend small urban farms.[6]

Graves's first step as proprietor of Cook's forfeited land was to convert the street railway from narrow to standard gauge. Almost his second, with owners of adjoining land—Washington Water Power, the Hypotheekbank, and Frank Hogan, a prominent real estate developer—was to offer eighty to ninety acres for a park on condition that the city build a winding, pretty drive and bring water to it. This would be Manito Park, named, its donors said, with the Nez Perce word for high ground. Manito would account for nearly half the parkland the city owned by 1908, and with its playfields, picnic areas, zoo, gardens, pond, and paths, it would become a favorite destination of many riders on Traction Company cars.[7]

To sell homesites, Graves hired an agent, Fred Grinnell—brusque, nervy, hammer and tongs. Grinnell touted the park, Manito Boulevard leading south with a parkway in its center, and twenty-minute service by Traction Company lines. Except for these features, the diagonal Grand Boulevard and streets that curved along the park boundaries, however, the district was laid out unimaginatively as a grid of rectangular blocks. "Extra large residential lots" facing the park went at $1,000. A few blocks away, inside lots sold for $200, corner lots for $250—with covenants requiring that homes on them cost at least $1,500. The farther from boulevards or park, the cheaper the site.[8]

As usual, Graves took care of his own: he sold his brother, Frank, fifty lots for $4,400, an average of $88, and Frank resold many to his friends to create an enclave of congenial neighbors of his choosing. A story goes that when someone pointed out that a high wall made Frank's own house look like a prison, he replied, "Jails build walls to keep the bastards in. I build walls to keep the bastards out!"[9]

Grinnell boasted that he would make Grand a "boulevard of maples," and Graves's men also planted 500 ornamental trees along the curving streets. (The advertising for Manito and other parklike districts fueled an imaginary rivalry between respectable northside working people and South Hill snobs who lived in mansions, owned businesses, and exploited city government. The fantasy has never died.) Between 1905 and 1910, Graves and those who either sold his land or relied on his trolleys to sell theirs established beautiful residential districts that shaped Spokane for half a century. Most of these are prized today as areas of fine old homes beside tree-lined streets.

As Spokane grew, Aubrey White came back from New York, an officer in Graves's railroad and real estate companies, aglow with the fervor of beautifying cities by rational planning, crying that Spokane must reserve its beauty spots for parkland before rising prices put them out of public reach. White's concern for parks was genuine, but by necessity—because the speculators owned the ground—he would work most closely with Graves and those who played Graves against the Washington Water Power Company for carlines. White, promoting vistas and parkways, introduced Spokane to the foremost landscape architects of the time, Olmsted Brothers of Brookline, Massachusetts.

White solicited John C. Olmsted to pause in Spokane enroute to Seattle to look at his south-side homesite. He also paid fifty dollars from his own pocket for what Olmsted called "advice of value . . . in your agitation for parks." Graves and several other real estate men pounced on the famous name as guaranteed to attract wealthy buyers; although it was too late to lay out Manito's residential tract, Graves engaged the firm to plan the park. John Olmsted, a kindly man who radiated quiet dignity, may have been dismayed by Graves's driving interest in selling land and by White's ebullient (and occasionally profane) push for parks. Because the firm was designing the site for Seattle's 1909 Alaska-Yukon-Pacific Exposition, Olmsted agreed that he or an associate, James Frederick Dawson, would stop for a day or two to confer with Spokane clients enroute to Seattle. Then White would haul him off to evaluate some remote spot in the city, chattering the while of parks, shrubs, flowers, and landscape design.[10]

During bumpy automobile or buggy rides, or sometimes struggles on foot through undergrowth, in districts about to be opened, Olmsted talked to White about a general plan for Spokane: he would connect the largest and finest parks by parkways and boulevards at least 150 feet wide so there might be "a distinct quality of luxury in width and beauty of turf and trees" for pleasure driving and walking. Houses must be set back, and land use restricted. Moreover, a system of diagonal avenues would save travel time and provide routes for rapid transit. The city's street railways in 1906 were "a disgrace," twisting, turning, trapped by narrow streets in grid plats and climbing steep hills where the city refused to condemn rights-of-way for suitable grades. Olmsted further mused that trees should be planted along residential streets. (Lewis Clark chaired a civic committee to plant trees along all streets.) Eventually, Olmsted and Dawson put their ideas in writing for the park board, but White suppressed this document for five years until the city passed a bond issue to buy parklands—had sellers realized the grand plan, land prices would have soared.[11]

White, of course, had to reveal the proposed boulevards and sites of future parks to developers when he cajoled them to donate land for parks and viewpoints. He firmly believed that wealthy men should give, not sell, parkland. Consequently, Graves, Hogan, Finch, Cowles, Lewis Clark, John Sherwood, Arthur Jones, and a good many others became privy to the Olmsted general design. Each could increase the potential value of his own ground knowing how it fit into the scheme.

Of these, Jones and Sherwood were not only property owners but preeminent real estate agents. Jones handled the Cowles properties. Sherwood was the Spokane agent for the Adams Real Estate Trust, which managed real estate bequeathed to the five children of Charles Francis Adams, son of John Quincy Adams, sixth president of the United States.[12]

Charles Francis Adams II, president of the Union Pacific Railroad, dreamed of making a fortune in western lands; he put all the money he could scrape up into real estate, buying heavily in Idaho, Portland, Oregon, and Spokane. An ambitious, abrasive man sunk in debt, Charles more or less dominated the family trust until his even more corrosive brother, Brooks Adams, elbowed him out to head off financial disaster. Both brothers owned commercial real estate in downtown Spokane independent of the family.

The Adamses had been buying Spokane land since 1889 through agents, and George Caspar Adams, a nephew of Charles and Brooks, had acquired more at foreclosure sales between 1890 and 1897. As a result, the Adams trust and the brothers owned most notably an undeveloped 640 acres in northwest Spokane, 900 in the southeast quarter of the city, 60 acres directly west of Manito Park surrounding an old sandpit and brickyard that had manufactured many of the bricks used in Spokane before the fire. Charles had mortgaged most of this ground to the family trust for loans to buy more land.[13]

In the climate of expansion after 1896, the Adamses proposed to sell off their land to developers at substantial profit. Streetcar lines would be a key to attracting buyers, so the Adamses watched with interest as Graves battled to enlarge Traction Company lines into a city-wide system, while the Washington Water Power Company protested that he invaded its territory. A WWP annual report noted that competition "has compelled a greater expenditure . . . than . . . ordinary conditions, and it is probable that additional lines will have to be built . . . to protect our interests," WWP advised stockholders.

When a sympathetic city council allowed Graves to build east on Third Avenue, the *Spokesman-Review* hailed his "signal victory." This eastward line, said Graves, would be a link in his original plan to reach Moran Prairie, southeast of the city, an area of small farms and orchards targeted for residential platting. WWP tried to smother Graves with a projected Spokane Southern Traction Company serving adjacent ground, the 900 acres owned by Charles Adams. It asserted that New York financiers and Adams backed the project.[14]

A few months later, the newspaper declared that "Graves has carried the street car fight . . . further into the enemy's territory" with a route toward Natatorium Park, the power company's destination park at the west end of Boone Avenue, and another competing line to Hillyard where Arthur Jones and Lewis Clark sold homesites for workingmen around the Great Northern shops. Along Summit Boulevard, winding atop the bluff above "Nat," Frank Hogan paid a premium for forty-seven lots and developed one of two elite housing sections on the north side before World War II. (The other was the Catholic enclave near Gonzaga College.) Next, Graves won a franchise for a route eastward on Main to the warehouse district, where he and F. A. Blackwell, originator of the Coeur d'Alene & Spokane Railway, spent $75,000 for a yard between the Northern Pacific and Great Northern freight terminals. With this acquisition, Graves sold the old terminal grounds on

Washington to Levi Hutton, who put up a building with his name on it.[15]

Both Graves and Washington Water Power now spent furiously. Both were deeply involved in other projects: Graves in Granby and an electric railway to the Palouse; the power company, which increased capital stock in 1903, in expanding its generating sites. When construction of a hydroelectric plant at Post Falls, Idaho, taxed its resources, WWP increased its capital stock again in April 1905 and borrowed $2 million, some of it for transmission lines into the Palouse country. For his part, Graves increased capital stock of the Traction Company to $1 million and in September 1905 floated a new bond issue secured by stock with the Title Guarantee and Trust Company of New York. Not long after, he merged the Traction Company with his electric railroad, the Spokane & Inland Empire.[16]

Neighborhood improvement clubs, got up for the betterment of distinct areas, were useful devices for promoting street railways. George M. Colborn, a Grinnell salesman, formed the Manito Park Improvement Club to endorse Graves's plans for that area. To a group calling themselves Citizens of the Fourth Ward, Dr. H. G. Mauzey, who had been recruited by Aubrey White, spoke for the Traction Company, declaring that he, for one, did "not believe it wise to turn down men . . . willing to spend their money" to build carlines through the ward. H. D. Skinner, a real estate broker, offered a resolution to the city council supporting Graves's application to build another route. Thus Graves gave political justification to a city council already inclined to favor him.[17]

And so it went. Graves ran carlines to settled sections already served by Washington Water Power and to new districts in northwest and southeast Spokane where street railways helped sell homesites. He held franchises, as well, to the fairgrounds (at Regal Street in a triangle formed by crossing railroad tracks) and to Recreation Park, about four blocks north of the fairgrounds, where the professional baseball team played. Graves had an interest in the team; for four years, he "sank a small fortune" in it. Graves also talked of building a destination park there, White City, financed by stock sales in a "distinct company . . . outside the Inland Empire system." But he declined to sign the five-year contract for current demanded by Washington Water Power and with sale of the baseball team, the amusement park scheme evaporated.[18]

In 1908, Graves asked for, and received, a blanket franchise for lines in every part of the city at the bargain fee of two mills a car mile. His man, Charles Liftchild, district manager for an insurance company, was said "to have the city council in hand," and after awarding the franchise, one councilman acknowledged that "the people would mob me" if he opposed the Traction Company. By this time, the lines of both street railway companies, sometimes laid across platted but vacant fields within a block or two of one another, stretched to every section of Spokane, and Graves's engineers were surveying an extension southeast to the Adams property that would become Lincoln Heights. WWP's twelve routes entered downtown principally on Howard Street, meeting at Riverside, and the Traction Company's twelve reached downtown by Washington Street, conjoining at Main, where the company had an information and ticket booth, before connecting with interurban trains at Main and Lincoln.[19]

The streetcar rivalry was hardly congenial, although neither company resorted to ripping up the other's tracks on dark nights as half a dozen competitors had in earlier days. In one noisy confrontation, Frank Graves, representing his brother's company, offered the city council $10,000, and then $15,000, for a track across the river bridge at Howard Street, successfully challenging WWP's claim to exclusive rights there. Then Jay Graves called on Henry Richards, WWP president, offering to buy the company's railways. Richards would not talk sale but was impressed by "the sublime cheek of the man . . . he is certainly clever and resourceful."[20]

And when John Finch, Frank Hogan, and John Sherwood opened Audubon and adjoining areas in northwest Spokane, Aubrey White bustled over the ground with them, wheedling a 150-foot parkway along the bluff overlooking the Spokane River. Graves presumed they had more or less agreed on a treed parkway and, in fact, released some railroad land for such an avenue. So he shouted angrily at Hogan and Sherwood in front of the city council when he discovered that he had been humbugged: the parkway—originally called Downriver but renamed Northwest Boulevard—had been moved back from the lip of the hill, and the developers supported Washington Water Power's request for a car track down its middle. (Sherwood was a WWP director.) It was one of the few times that Graves lost his poise in public. He had to be satisfied with a zigzag route north of the park (Audubon) that Finch and Hogan donated.

In the ensuing months Graves would be so aggressive in northwest Spokane that Henry Richards asked Howard Elliott, president of the Northern Pacific, to rein him in, explaining that Graves's vindictive tactics would "seriously affect the business of our lines, not now remunerative. . . . We feel, as pioneers in the district, we should be permitted to enjoy the loss undisturbed. . . . Leave us alone in our misery."[21]

Street railways to new districts spurred land speculation, an expanding market generating its own momentum. Graves not only opened two of Spokane's prestigious anchor districts, Manito Park and Rockwood, but also, for additions he did not market, usually built the street railways: east on Seventeenth to additions that Grinnell sold near Mount Vernon and Ray streets, to Lincoln Heights, to Arthur Jones's Cannon Hill Park, north to Corbin Park, and northwest to Audubon. The Washington Water Power Company also laid new lines, expanding from 42 miles in 1903 to 109 by 1910.[22]

Spokane's boosters crowed that the city was growing 10 percent a year, and a good many of them rode the boom to wealth. Between 1900 and 1910, the population rose from roughly 37,000 to more than 104,000. A majority of new arrivals were between twenty-five and forty-four years old, men with families looking for stable employment and homes. In December 1907, Spokane nearly doubled its land area by annexations north, east, and south. New districts needed carlines, and in a time when most families shopped downtown, merchants competed for storefronts near loading zones. Spokane was on a building binge, and while WWP grumbled that "the demand for increased or improved service" was "greater than the available patronage warranted," it kept pace. Building permits rose from 1,494 worth $2.4 million in 1903 to 2,927 worth $5.9 million in 1908; in the next year, although the number barely increased, the value leaped to $8.7 million in commercial and residential permits. That was the high point until the forties.[23]

Some districts were developed almost exclusively for families of day laborers and artisans—Hillyard, Union Park, Peaceful Valley, College Avenue, and the courthouse district. There contractors occasionally built cheap frame four-room houses with dirt half-cellars, or real estate speculators put up a few houses to be rented or sold. (Sillman brothers, who later built a hotel, started this

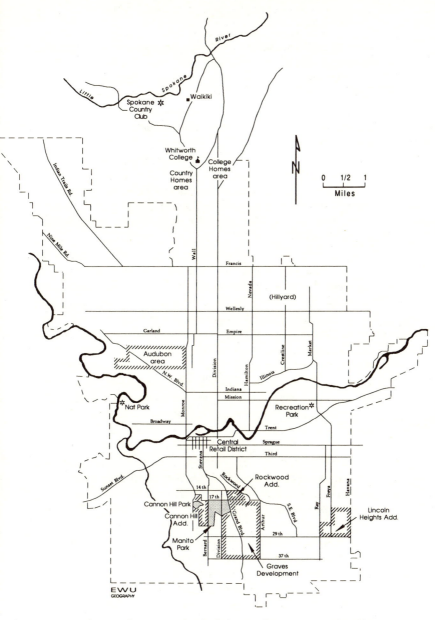

MAP 1. Spokane and vicinity. The shaded areas show Manito and Rockwood districts developed by Graves, and Cannon Hill and Lincoln Heights, made practical by his streetcar routes. To the north are the areas Graves promoted around Whitworth College, his estate Waikiki, and the Spokane Country Club. (*By David Anderson, Eastern Washington University*)

way.) Union Park and Peaceful Valley, virtually on the valley floor, flooded in wet seasons.

If carlines were a convenience for new residential areas (and Graves willingly took workmen's nickels for his trolleys), water was essential. The city government strove to supply water to a city moving outward with the relentless pull of an ebbing tide. Spokane's water system fell farther behind residential expansion and deeper in debt. Developers installed their own water distribution systems and invented gambits to bring city water to their ground; Graves specified that the city must water Manito Park as his condition for giving it; Hogan and Finch similarly tied their gift of Audubon Park to city water. The private systems, drawing from wells or springs, were eventually sold to the city.

Water, even when supplied, was nearly always short. Engineers protested that homeowners wasted it sprinkling lawns and gardens, and the council imposed periodic rationing. Some businesses installed water meters to measure costs as early as 1889, but when the council decreed in 1905 that houses must put in meters, citizens balked. Water "has made Spokane a beautiful city," the recently rich Emeline (Mrs. Charles) Sweeny sniffed. "I drive visitors to see the north side where workingmen have their little homes, green lawns, and vineclad cottages." Browne's Addition, she went on, once glittered with electric lights, but when Washington Water Power installed meters, the "lights went out." Nevertheless, the city put in water meters as annual consumption gushed from 2.8 billion gallons in 1900 to more than 11.3 billion by 1910.[24]

There had been some sentiment in the state's large cities for turning over water and parks to nonpartisan citizen commissions. Spokane voters amended the city charter in May 1907 to authorize local improvement districts for utilities and streets and to create a park commission. For the park board, the mayor appointed ten men, who promptly elected Aubrey White president. They "resolved to govern the parks as closely along business lines as possible," and one member, Charles Liftchild, moved that they employ "some eminent landscape artist." Frank Hogan, who had outfoxed Graves in the Audubon streetcar matter, chaired the acquisitions committee. White now had his mandate for parks; he could bring Olmsted out of the closet, so to speak, along with the park system they had talked about.[25]

With John Olmsted or Fred Dawson at hand, David Brown,

the dairyman, hired Olmsted Brothers to lay out Rockwood, an addition east of Manito Park, which he was developing for Brooks Adams. Graves's Spokane-Washington Improvement Company had quietly bought up the area adjoining Rockwood and now employed the Olmsted firm to design it as an extension of Rockwood.

Graves's company surveyed the route for a street railway and replatted the area according to Olmsted recommendations. White took John Olmsted to see it: hilly, rocky, and overgrown, it had a jutting knob of rock several acres wide. Despite a jolting automobile ride over narrow cart tracks through dense second-growth pine, Olmsted saw in Graves's land possibilities for contoured streets and fine hillside homesites.

To Olmsted White expounded that Graves's "land company is worked in conjunction with his electric railway company, being composed in the main of the same stockholders. The idea is to get hold of dead but promising land secretly and as cheaply as possible, then to lay out some streets with better grades and build an electric railway through the property, advertise it and sell off lots at good prices and as rapidly as possible." White himself thought of building a home here, "partly with a view to helping boom this land." Olmsted merely remarked that White might have difficulty keeping servants contented that far from town.[26]

To "boom" land, as White put it, some real estate companies ran touring autos along downtown streets; barkers offered to drive prospects immediately to see homesites. Grinnell closed sixty-two sales in Manito Park in one month for an average of $432 a lot. (Graves set sales quotas, offering a hat and a suit to anyone who met them.) In every part of the city, brokers claimed brisk sales.

Olmsted counseled Brown to hold his Rockwood lots "for profit in the rise in value which is most likely to occur after the proposed boulevard has been constructed, the street railway has been put in operation and several houses of good class built in the immediate neighborhood." Indeed, the winding boulevard through the Adams and the Graves properties would be the most celebrated roadway in Spokane for the next thirty years. Other Adams ground would come on the market as prices rose.

Although the Adamses only occasionally visited Spokane, they rallied to the city's causes. Charles wrote U.S. senators in support of Spokane's bid for a military post, not entirely an altruistic gesture, for Sherwood pointed out that northwest Spokane would benefit from "a diagonal boulevard, and electric [railway] line, city water and lights [that] would follow" location of the post, "thereby animating what is now a dreary forest," and presumably increase the value of the Adams Trust's 640 acres there. Brooks, who had been writing on the public obligations of trusts and railroads, joined the attorneys who represented Spokane merchants before the Interstate Commerce Commission to argue again for terminal railroad rates.[27]

While Jay Graves's people stepped briskly to plat and advertise their part of the Rockwood area, David Brown dragged his feet. A pragmatic, stubborn man, "he is cautious and carefully studies everything," Olmsted observed, "and knows by experience that he is liable to think of something better later." Brown re-drew Olmsted's layouts of "curvilinear" streets and then drew them again, while Graves's men graded streets and laid macadam on Rockwood Boulevard. Olmsted thought the paving "poor" and the railway grade too steep, inartistic, typical of engineers. Brown agreed the lots should be large—he had friends who wanted big lots—until Grinnell warned that they might cost too much and advised him to sell two lots to anyone who wanted a big site. Graves's company planted trees along his streets; the prospective park superintendent, John W. Duncan, put in shrubs. Graves sold inside lots at $2,000 or $3,000 and a choice corner for as much as $8,000, and still Brown deliberated. Nearly a year passed before he grudgingly mailed the maps to Boston for Brooks Adams's approval so the work could commence.[28]

When it was done, Rockwood would be a showplace of hillside sites overlooking streets curved to the terrain, with striking houses set well back, broad lawns, and great trees. The street railway rode a parklike shoulder alongside the boulevard. An address on Rockwood instantly identified one as a south-side brahmin.

Meanwhile, Arthur D. Jones organized the Cannon Hill Park Company with John Finch and W. H. Cowles to develop the Adams Trust's sixty acres directly west of Manito Park. Much of Cannon Hill Park was hilly and had underlying rock near the surface. To market it to best advantage, Jones offered the city some thirteen acres around the pond as Adams Park, promising to spend $2,000 for improvements if the park board would spend $4,000. He implied that Charles Adams II was donating the park. The board accepted; it would enlarge the pond by dredging, plant trees, and eventually construct an elaborate concrete wading pool with arched bridges carved out of native rock and canoes. It also renamed the place Cannon Hill Park.

On Olmsted's advice, Jones agreed to a wide parkway [Twenty-first Avenue] leading directly to Manito Park. Olmsted designed seventeen prime blocks facing the park as a curvilinear section for expensive homes. South of Twenty-first, Cannon Hill Park Addition reverted to the usual rectangular grid blocks. The Washington Water Power Company's street railway ran on Monroe past the western boundary of Cannon Hill Park; the Traction Company's, on Bernard at its eastern edge.[29]

Jones estimated that park-front lots would sell for $1,250 but after one week exulted that thirty in various locations sold for an average of $1,400. The first house in the addition, a two-story English style on Oneida, cost $6,570. Another, $20,000. By comparison, Rockwood homes averaged $16,000, although one reportedly cost $48,000. If the houses were not as showy and the lots not as large as in Rockwood, Cannon Hill Park homes nonetheless were among the fairest in the city, although the residents soon encountered freezing pipes due to the difficulty of digging trenches deep in the rocky ground. And a few stores came in, against restrictions but with the consent of neighbors.[30]

While Jones opened Cannon Hill Park, John S. and William C. Malloy offered to buy the 640 Adams acres in northwest Spokane to develop as irrigated tracts. The brothers had promoted irrigation near Hayden Lake, homesites at Ponderay, Idaho, and the South Side Cable Addition to Spokane named for an old cable railway. They called the Adams section Boulevard Park and predicted they could sell it all within a year. With the trust's approval, Sherwood gave the brothers an option, writing Charles Adams that "the fact that Mr. Graves has a right of way of 14 acres . . . which he purchased of us a year ago, was the main consideration on [the Malloys'] part in taking the option."[31]

The Malloys abandoned their plan for irrigation, however, and eight months later turned over their Boulevard Park Realty Company to new stockholders headed by Samuel Glasgow, founder, secretary-treasurer, and Spokane manager for the Centennial Mill Company. The new stockholders assumed the Malloys' debt to the Adams Trust.[32]

The last large unimproved Adams property sold before the Malloy option: the 900 acres in southeast Spokane—Lincoln Heights—was sold, and once more Graves's Spokane Traction Company was pivotal, for this land lay more than three miles from downtown. It was said to be the largest addition platted to Spokane to that time. Graves surveyed to extend his Rockwood line eastward on the general path of Twenty-second Avenue to Southeast Boulevard and then along it southeast to Twenty-ninth in Lincoln Heights.

Haughty Charles himself returned to Spokane to close the sale to developers, arriving with a princely flourish, and spoke at a banquet in Louis Davenport's Hall of the Doges for 135 boosters of a park system. He recounted his experiences as the first president of the Boston park commission, and the evening ended with an enthusiastic endorsement of a proposed million-dollar bond issue for Spokane's parks.[33]

Adams sold the Lincoln Heights property to William H. Kiernan and Jay Lawyer, partners in the Western Trust and Investment Company. Lawyer wanted to hire the Olmsted Brothers because, John Olmsted assumed, he liked the firm's work on Graves's rock-strewn additions and wanted similar "curviliniar streets for this rocky, wooded tract." One piece had been tentatively set aside as Rockwood Park, but Lawyer doubted (correctly) that the park board could afford it; nonetheless, he hoped to use that name—capitalizing on the glitter of the original Rockwood—for his addition. But it was soon Lincoln Heights.[34]

The Graves brothers knew Lawyer well and doubtless heard his plans for Lincoln Heights before negotiations concluded with Adams. Will Graves acted as trustee for Lawyer's personal real estate and as his attorney in Lawyer's separation from his wife. As soon as the Adams sale was sure, the Traction Company began laying track along a 60-foot right-of-way from Rockwood to the Kiernan-Lawyer ground on the line of Twenty-second with an understanding that the route could be widened into a 120-foot parkway.[35]

Not only trolley service but the city's water system made this a propitious time to open Lincoln Heights. The city served south Spokane from its Upriver Station, pumping to four standpipes, one of them in Lincoln Heights, with an auxiliary pumping station at Twenty-fourth and Ray in the heart of the Kiernan-Lawyer development. But city sewers stopped half a mile from Lincoln Heights.

Even with sewer pipe buried in its streets, the addition opened with septic tanks, still awaiting connection to the city system. Prospective buyers often drove iron rods into the ground to test for subsurface rock before agreeing to buy a lot.[36]

John Olmsted was not much taken with Lincoln Heights: the street railway would render lots on its route "noisy and citified," and the part east of Southeast Boulevard, "graded as a country road," promised no vistas; it was "useless . . . to run curved streets through it as it will probably be cheap lots and purchasers of these mostly prefer straight streets." He found some rocks as high as a three-story house. The park commission had already spoken for the best views, the rocky bluffs east of Southeast Boulevard, and Spokane Traction built in haste on straight lines, ignoring the natural features; it ran through a pond that Olmsted hoped to preserve as a small residential lake. The pond would be dredged for its fertile earth to start lawns, as Jones had done at Cannon Hill Park, and then filled.[37]

Although they had already sold 400 lots, Kiernan and Lawyer inaugurated Lincoln Heights with gala tours, sending tickets to more than 4,000 to ride the new Traction Company line on November 6 and 7, 1909. The visitors saw a raw countryside cut by rough street grades, curbs and sidewalks, and wooden stakes with colored ribbons stirring in the fall breeze to mark lots. Gordon C. Corbaley, once secretary of the chamber of commerce and a Jones salesman, predicted that 1909 was "the year" for southside expansion and that buyers' interest would center on Lincoln Heights. "With street car transportation and all modern conveniences . . . [there is] no good reason why a big community should not build up" there. Through the winter and into the spring, the curious rode the streetcars to see Lincoln Heights. Real estate men trumpeted that on sunny days a thousand came, and asserted that "the carline extension . . . regarded as a doubtful venture, [is] already a revenue payer." The Traction Company ran as many as seventy-four cars a day and doubled service on Sundays when, it was claimed, 2,500 rode.[38]

As Lincoln Heights flowered, much of it as garden tracts, Graves lost his monarchial command of the Traction Company when he sold it as a division of the Spokane & Inland Empire. Although at the time the company showed an operating profit, Will Graves told the state board of equalization that "the stocks of the Graves companies are not worth a cent, because they are paying no dividends and their values are purely speculative." Jay Graves was no longer able to stretch new carlines to new additions on his whim: his free-wheeling days of building where he pleased had ended.[39]

With the sale, Henry Richards of WWP resorted again to writing the buyers, Howard Elliott and Jim Hill, about competition from Graves, and Elliott tried to soothe him by explaining that Hill, who set policy, had not given Graves authority to build more streetcar lines. Then Elliott warned Graves of his feeling that "we ought not to be fighting with Richards, unless there are some very good reasons." Graves responded warmly: "Richards has always objected to everything we have done . . . but I have not considered his objections at any time in the past and do not think we should at this time. . . . I feel that the building up of our property is the proper direction." Richards considered his ideas "dreams," he went on, airing his conviction that to remain competitive and profitable, the Traction Company should extend to growing new sections. He pointed out that property owners on north Howard had guaranteed the $4,500 cost of their carline. He could not renege on them, he said, and "as things stand now I have to answer many questions about future earnings to friends who invested through me."[40]

Graves's departure from the Traction Company coincided, although he could not realize it then, with the slowing of immigration and the onset of a general languor in business. As immigration lost momentum, home sales stagnated. David Brown's indecision had been fatal to his hopes for large profits in Rockwood. Building permits in Spokane fell in 1912 by half from 1911, and by half again in 1913; the year 1914 would be the slowest before 1933. In its enthusiasm, Spokane had overbuilt.

Street railways faced particular difficulties. Patronage fell after 1910, and in 1912, for the first time, the phrase "probably attributable to the increasing use of automobiles" appeared in the Washington Water Power Company's annual report, to be repeated each year until it became trite. The Spokane Traction Company "made a good showing . . . by comparison with Washington Water Power," an officer maintained, but "we are not earning 8 percent interest on the investment" as Elliott and Hill demanded. Longer routes ran at losses.[41]

Early in 1922, Spokane citizens approved a franchise for a consolidated streetcar system, and on July 1, 1922, Washington Water Power merged all carlines as Spokane United Railways. For years thereafter, it subsidized the trolleys with revenues from power sales.

Real estate continued to sell slowly. Brokers usually had a triumph for the *Spokesman-Review*'s Sunday real estate section, but the vacant plats did not fill. In 1911 the city commenced foreclosures on delinquent assessments; it would be selling these derelict lots until World War II. In a languishing housing market, booster optimism faded.

The Olmsteds dunned David Brown until 1912 to pay them for planning Rockwood, not encouraged by the engineer, Otto A. Weile, who confessed that he had collected from Brown only by refusing to pay his milk bill until it evened out with the money Brown owed him. Finally, Carl A. Shuff, once manager of the Spokane-Washington Improvement Company, persuaded Brown to settle his account.

The Adams Trust threatened foreclosure for the balance due on Cannon Hill Park, and when Arthur Jones offered a compromise, John Sherwood, agent for the trust, advised the Adamses that "W. H. Cowles, a very wealthy man, is interested with Mr. Jones in this land," recommending they hold out for the original terms. Jones paid.

On June 29, 1918, Jay Graves offered at auction the 400 unsold lots in the Manito Park and Rockwood districts, valued at approximately $1.4 million. Roughly one-third, 110 lots, sold for only $56,000. Sixty years later, one could still find a vacant lot facing Rockwood Boulevard.[42]

Several years after Graves's sell-off, Grinnell, as agent, auctioned nearly 200 lots unsold in Lincoln Heights, lots that in 1910 commanded as much as $800. In 1922 they went for between $35 and $120, depending on size and location.[43]

And so, the boom days passed. In the explosive rush to house the burgeoning population of Spokane, street railways had played their significant role in shaping the city. Jay Graves had built wherever there were houses to be sold, and he had forced the water power company to compete in serving every corner of the city. Graves, and the men who relied on his trolleys, had left their indelible stamp in parks, treed avenues, streets curved to the shape of the terrain, and stately homes.

CHAPTER 4

The Electric Railway

Less than a month before Jay Graves took control of the Montrose street railway, Frederick A. Blackwell, a quiet, self-made lumberman with extensive stumpage in north Idaho, organized a company to build an electric railway between Coeur d'Alene, Idaho, and Spokane. Blackwell was believed to have a traffic arrangement with, and perhaps covert financial help from, the Union Pacific through a subsidiary, the Oregon Railway & Navigation Company; he meant to capitalize on the expanding lumber business and on the widespread dissatisfaction among lumbermen and merchants with the Northern Pacific's service to the Coeur d'Alene area. Blackwell bargained with Graves for a connection with the Montrose that would give his railway access to downtown Spokane. With Blackwell in his pocket, so to speak, Graves had reorganized the Montrose as the Spokane Traction Company. Soon the two, Blackwell and Graves, were going out together to solicit subscriptions to the new Coeur d'Alene road.[1]

The president of the Northern Pacific, Charles S. Mellen, tried to stop the project; his attorneys, on instructions, opposed track crossings to lumber mills and a franchise to enter Spokane. The Union Pacific, on the other hand, delivered rails and equipment to Blackwell at reduced rates and pledged rebates on lumber shipments to midwestern markets. And Graves hinted that James J. Hill himself was friendly, although Hill's son, Louis, protested that the Hills made Graves no promises. Graves and Jim Hill had talked privately, however, and who could say what passed between them?[2]

Blackwell laid rail to Spokane, crossing the Northern Pacific line four times, and had the Coeur d'Alene & Spokane Railway in operation by December 1903. The first passenger train used two old open summer cars borrowed from Washington Water Power, the sides closed with canvas tarpaulins—a chilly ride. A bottle of warming Old Crow whiskey made its rounds among the adult passengers. Blackwell's road hauled light freight and passengers by electric train in the daytime and lumber by steam locomotive at night. Mellen grouched that it could never have been built but for "assistance and promises" from the Union Pacific in breach of a territorial compact.[3]

Soon Graves and Blackwell were planning an extension of Blackwell's electric into the Palouse country, territory the Northern Pacific regarded as belonging to it. "You understand," a western railroad man informed Howard Elliott, now president of the NP, "that Jay P. Graves of the Spokane Traction Company practically controls the Coeur d'Alene and Spokane Railway." Graves prowled eastern financial houses showing plans for an interurban system, implying that Jim Hill stood behind him in some unspecified way. To bankers, Hill's interest seemed reasonable. He would gain Palouse traffic.[4]

State-chartered trust companies in the East, engaging in a wide range of finance including trusteeship for bond issues, were eager for new business, and Graves obviously wakened some interest. He organized the Spokane & Inland Railway company on December 13, 1904, to build railways and electrical generating plants in Washington and Idaho. (It swallowed his paper Spokane Interurban and absorbed the Coeur d'Alene & Spokane.) The directors included Lewis Clark, Jay's brother Will, Blackwell, and Alfred Coolidge, president of the Traders National Bank, Spokane. Coolidge and his partner, A. Fielding McClaine, owned banks and lands in the Palouse; his name seemed a sure sign that Graves was headed into the Palouse. Graves, moreover, was among the bank's large borrowers and may have gotten his initial capital from three Traders loans: $50,000 for the Spokane Terminal Company, $25,000 for Spokane Traction, and $50,000 more for the Spokane & Inland. He organized the terminal company to construct a central station in Spokane on March 1, 1905; it, too, was authorized to build and operate interurban railroads.[5]

In sounding out bond possibilities, Graves apparently had been rebuffed by the Boston financier Henry Lee Higginson, recently elected a director of Granby Consolidated, and Howard Elliott tried to cut him off from other bond houses. Elliott asked Robert Bacon of J. P. Morgan and Company to "discourage" investors from backing Graves. A Palouse road "is a bad scheme for our interests," Elliott told Bacon, "and, in my judgment, will be a bad scheme for anyone to put money into because the territory cannot support three railroads."[6]

Elliott was too late. The investment bankers E. H. Rollins and Sons of Boston, and Peabody, Houghteling and Company of Chicago had sent George W. Ristine, an expert on railroads, to evaluate a route proposed by Graves. (When Graves's surveyor fell ill, Gustav A. Hensel, Great Northern surveyor, took over the work.) Graves told Ristine that Jim Hill had seen his maps and that he assumed, if he himself could not arrange financing, Hill would introduce him to some friends who would be interested. Ristine discovered that "negotiations have so far progressed [with Rollins and Peabody] that it would be embarrassing and entirely useless . . . to discourage the investment." Jay Graves had his money without Hill's friendly intervention, and he had convinced bond sellers to support him before they sent their man west to see what he was talking about.

Graves's route, approved by Ristine, ran southward from Spokane to the farm and forest industries of the Palouse. In his favor, Graves was riding, bouyant as a surfer, on a wave of interurban railway construction that attracted investors. The securities of interurbans in heavily populated areas were regarded as moderate risks with good returns. And Graves went about financing his railroad in an acceptable way: most interurbans were built from the proceeds of bond sales while their promoters took the capital stock either to hold or sell, thus "rewarding themselves without the risk of their funds," as one analyst put it. Many interurbans, moreover, carried a certain amount of "water" in capitalization. In 1905 interurban electrics were being built in many parts of the West. There were, for instance, lines at Bellingham and Yakima in Washington, and to the southwest the expanding Oregon Electric connected Portland to Salem and Forest Grove.[7]

Graves held a unique advantage: his suburban lines carried passengers into the heart of downtown Spokane by connecting with Traction Company routes. (A good many interurbans in other cities terminated on the outskirts because purchase of rights-of-way was too expensive in built-up areas or because local ordinances restricted their operation in crowded districts.) In entering the Palouse, Graves could drive directly to established towns; he did not need to prove the traffic of the country. Most residents of the Palouse felt, at the time, that the Northern Pacific and Union Pacific served them poorly. As one old-timer observed, the NP "hugs too close to the mountains to reach the whole country. . . . Colfax is too far distant to ship over any branch of the NP . . . [and] is at the mercy of the Union Pacific."[8]

As he built his railroad, Graves expected to plant new suburbs where businessmen, whisked to Spokane by electric for the day's toil, might retire at eventide to restore their spirits on small acreages. The agrarian background of Graves's generation still attracted men to the soil. Even Graves fancied himself at ease in quiet countryside, lulled by birdcalls.

For this real estate development, Graves formed yet another company, the Railway Land and Improvement Company, on October 2, 1905, with Coolidge, his real estate associates Fred Grinnell and Arthur Jones, Waldo G. Paine, railroad traffic manager, and Denis D. Twohy, one of the Twohy brothers, railroad contractors, who had purchased the Old National Bank. The firm would plat unsettled valleys as New Home, Moran, Valleyford, Ochlare, Mount Hope, and so on. At Valleyford, sixteen miles from Spokane, Jones advertised five-acre tracts for $750 that "will do away with fears of the landlord and make you independent. . . . Live in Valleyford and work in town." Grinnell offered five-, ten-, or twenty-acre tracts at Ochlare "for that class of people who do business in the city . . . and want freedom from the city noise, dust, dirt, and taxes."[9]

Paine, who left a grocery business for the Coeur d'Alene & Spokane, fronted as president of Railway Land and Improvement. When it was time for selling land, the company amended its articles three times in twelve days to expand its purposes to include irrigation, and it raised its capital stock to pay for sidewalks, street grading, and promotion of unborn towns.

Some merchants in established towns, campaigning hard against mail-order competitors, now feared that Graves's railway would steal their customers for Spokane. The *Pullman Tribune* put their apprehensions into print, but the *Colfax Commoner* sniffed that an electric railway was "inevitable," that only "unprogressive" merchants stood to lose trade, and added smugly that "whatever develops . . . will help Colfax." At a town meeting—one of many—to solicit subscriptions for his road, Graves exacted $12,000 from Colfax citizens; he asked Pullman for a subsidy, too; smaller places, like Garfield, he pinched for free right-of-way. Rosalia granted right-of-way and a forty-year nonexclusive franchise for electric current and lights. Railroad subsidies were common demands. Towns expected them.[10]

Graves offered frequent service that would allow rural patrons to commute for business and pleasure and speed the delivery of goods from Spokane wholesalers to country retailers. Unfortunately, local traffic was usually the least profitable business of interurban railroading; a line could be very busy yet not make a profit. Without discouraging passengers and packages, Graves's people strove to take the larger traffic: machinery, lumber, grain, and other major freight. In each of the larger towns of the Palouse, the leading businessmen, bankers, and politicians resolved that the railroad would line their pockets, too. Consequently, the Spokane & Inland encountered little real opposition to subsidies or rights-of-way.

Before many bonds were sold, Graves started building. A Spokane Chamber of Commerce subscription campaign, headed by David T. Ham, raised about $200,000. The railroad's directors—Graves, Will Graves, Clark, Blackwell, and Coolidge—were said to have chipped in another $200,000, evidently $40,000 each. Jay Graves apparently used funds from selling some Granby stock, and $40,000 is probably all the cash that he, or any other director, invested in the Spokane & Inland. With this meager bankroll, much in paper pledges, Graves contracted with Porter Brothers, Spokane, to build twenty-two miles to Waverly where the railroad man D. C. Corbin owned a sugar beet factory and orchards had been planted. Graves bought enough ties, however, to reach Moscow.[11]

As surveyed, the Spokane & Inland would follow valleys southeast from Spokane to Waverly, and then veer almost directly south, emerging from piney scablands into the unique dunes of the Palouse country. At Spring Valley, a town to be established, it would split into Colfax and Moscow divisions; the Colfax line would touch Rosalia, Thornton, and Steptoe; the Moscow would serve Oakesdale, Garfield, and Palouse City. (There were to be a number of new shipping points, and Grinnell and Blackwell stations.) At Palouse City, the Moscow division would meet the Potlatch Lumber Company's railroad into Idaho timberlands. As much as any reasonably direct route could, the Spokane & Inland drove through the heart of the Palouse. Graves intended, at some future time, to push from Moscow on to Lewiston.

Where his electric entered a town already served by the NP or the OR&N, Graves stipulated, in his demand for subsidy, that his depot ground be as near the others as possible.

In choosing a power system for his railroad, Graves showed that flair for innovation that so impressed his admirers in Spokane. Rather than the usual three-phase electric, he chose the novel single-phase motor only recently perfected by the Westinghouse Electric and Manufacturing Company. His 1,200-horsepower locomotives were, consequently, among the first single-phase used in the United States. The new system called attention to the Spokane road in eastern investment houses because it was the same one adopted for a thirty-one-mile section of the New York, New Haven & Hartford to provide a smokeless and ashless approach to Grand Central Station in New York City.[12]

The Spokane & Inland bought all its current from Washington Water Power, delivered by a three-phase line to a frequency-changing station, a romanesque brick building near Liberty Park in Spokane. There the current was converted to 45,000 volt alternating and fed over copper wires to fifteen substations along the route. The substations, squarish, unadorned brick-and-concrete structures, stepped down the voltage to 6,600 and sent this over wires to locomotives and self-propelled passenger cars that drew electricity by trolley poles or pantographs.[13]

Self-propelled passenger cars were powered by four 100-horsepower motors underneath connected to the trucks. The cars could be hooked in tandem, and operated as one, for larger passenger capacity; they could hit speeds of thirty-five to forty miles an hour in open country—a velocity that seemed rocketlike to patrons used to horses and wagons. Both passenger and freight trains reduced power to pass along city streets in Spokane.

Graves's choice of motive power and the way he built the Spokane & Inland show that he was guided by men familiar with the interurban business, perhaps Ristine, the investment bankers' man, and Benjamin J. Weeks, an experienced electric railroad man whom Graves hired as general manager. (Clyde would learn under Weeks.) For the most part, however, the Spokane & Inland emerged as an electric interurban typical for its time.

In many parts of the nation, interurbans owned amusement parks to promote summer and holiday travel. The Spokane & Inland opened beaches and parks at Liberty, Hayden, and Coeur d'Alene lakes. Both Graves and Lewis Clark built homes at Hayden. The Traction and Coeur d'Alene lines transferred passengers from one to the other, so that a Spokane family, wearied of the city, could take a streetcar, connect with an interurban, speed to the lake in the morning and be home by evening.

Blackwell himself held twenty acres of waterfront at Coeur d'Alene lake, which the railroad designated Blackwell Park. David Ham, who had led the Spokane subscription drive for Graves, formed the Liberty Lake Land Company to operate a thirty-two-acre park, Wicomico—with beaches, boat rental, dance hall, concessions, and depot—at Liberty, "only 40 minutes from Spokane." (Right-of-way was no barrier there, for Arthur Jones owned large tracts near Liberty; he would farm one as a hobby most of his life.) A new Hayden Lake Improvement Company acquired buildings and 140 acres for a hotel, dining room, and golf course. Its board elected Aubrey White president.[14]

As the railroad took shape, Graves hired an advertising man to feed items and photographs to country and city newspapers. The stories told of subsidies from towns along the line, "theater specials" from Spokane at Saturday midnight, nine bungalow-style depots with conical towers designed by the Spokane architect Albert Held, surveys to Lewiston, and a possible extension into Oregon. The advertising man also arranged photo displays in many cities showing the country served by the railroad—pictures "vivid enough," said an editor, "to make any onlooker accept Horace Greeley's advice to 'go west.'"[15]

Graves not only talked of extending the line to Lewiston but perhaps into the Big Bend, that arid plateau in the great sweep of the Columbia River. From time to time, he talked to reporters about it, and his surveyors stalked the countryside.

These ambitious plans vexed Howard Elliott of the Northern Pacific, who worried that if the Spokane & Inland "build all the lines they are talking about, they will be in a position to handle grain and lumber both from Spokane to a connection with the Canadian Pacific and to a connection with the Milwaukee . . . which will put the Canadian Pacific and the St. Paul roads into this Palouse-Lewiston country." (The Graves line could join Corbin's new Spokane International to the CPR; the Milwaukee was surveying through northern Idaho.) Elliott hoped that "some arrangement could be made to control the Spokane & Inland, such as was talked over last autumn by Mr. Baker and others on a trip west." Baker was George F. Baker, Jr., of the First National Bank, New York, a Hill man.[16]

While Elliott fretted, the Spokane & Inland gasped for money to keep building, tided over hand-to-mouth by a succession of promissory notes—thirty in all—to the First Trust and Savings, Chicago, for $25,000 each. The Coeur d'Alene & Spokane division made money, a net of $64,877 in 1905 and double its 1905 first quarter at the start of 1906, but not enough to keep Graves going.[17]

One, perhaps the only, avenue to more money for the railroad would be to form a new company to sell securities. Grinnell would say, later on, that the investors persuaded Graves to consolidate to bring in new capital. Consequently, Graves organized the Inland Empire Railway Company on January 15, 1906, with articles authorizing it to build and operate steam and electric railroads between Spokane and stations in Washington, Idaho, Oregon, and British Columbia and to buy or develop electrical generating plants in the same places. On April 21, the directors changed the company's name to the Spokane & Inland Empire Railroad Company. Capitalized for $10 million (100,000 shares at $100 par), the Spokane & Inland Empire acquired, by stock exchanges, the Spokane Traction, Coeur d'Alene & Spokane, Spokane & Inland, and Spokane Terminal companies, taking their properties, franchises, and debts.[18]

All of the 100,000 shares in the Spokane & Inland Empire were subscribed: Jay Graves took 45,000; Blackwell and Clark, 25,000 each; and Aaron Kuhn, Paine, W. C. Davidson, and Will Graves, lesser amounts. Kuhn, the onetime Palouse moneylender and merchant now associated with Coolidge and McClaine in the Traders National Bank, succeeded Coolidge as a railroad director.

These men did not invest new money. At a directors' meeting on January 19 in one of the Fernwell Building rooms that housed Frank Graves's legal firm and all of Jay Graves's companies, Blackwell paid for his 25,000 by turning over 4,000 shares of the Spokane & Inland and 16,500 of the short-lived Inland Empire "to be disposed of" by the company, and by donating his services as an officer. Clark followed with a similar pledge, then Jay Graves, and each of the others in turn, handing over stock in the subsumed companies. With this rite, the stock of each man in the Spokane & Inland Empire, noted the secretary, "was deemed paid in full."[19]

The directors elected Blackwell chairman, Jay Graves president, and Clark vice-president. Actually, Blackwell had more or less decamped. Relegated to a figurehead by Graves, he turned to his plans for a new steam railroad from Coeur d'Alene into northeastern

Washington. Then the board voted to give the executive committee (Blackwell, Graves, and Clark) authority to issue up to $6 million in "preferred rights." Except for Jay Graves and his closest associates, no one seemed to comprehend that "rights" was not another term for stock. And in future Spokane & Inland Empire balance sheets, preferred rights were never shown in the debt column, so that assets regularly appeared greater than their real value.[20]

The railroad now had paper to sell that would bring in $16 million at par—although it never sold at par—and Jay and Will Graves set out for the East to sell. The bloom was fading on electrics, and it was slow going. They moved some common stock by giving it away to those who bought preferred rights. As he had before, Jay Graves went to see Jim Hill.

At Hill's request, Graves wrote him a personal prospectus four pages long: "I am of the opinion that the electrical railways owned by this Company will have sufficient earnings in themselves to pay the dividends on all the outstanding up to 7%," he said, mentioning the "growth of the country" as another inducement to investing, and offered Hill preferred rights at par and common shares amounting to one-half the number of preferred rights bought—the standard deal. He asked Hill for $500,000 to tide over the railroad for the coming month and closed: "I have a large investment, for me, in these enterprises, and expect to invest more as I have the utmost confidence in their success."[21]

Whatever Hill thought of Graves's proposition, he knew that a friendly tie with the Spokane & Inland Empire would guarantee the Great Northern traffic from the Palouse. He apparently bought 21,000 shares of common—one-fifth of the voting power—and tucked them quietly out of sight in the Lake Superior Company, Ltd., a Michigan partnership association that he used for business the Great Northern could not conduct under its charter. (The existence of the Lake Superior Company would slip out in Hill's testimony before a Minnesota legislative committee in February 1907, generating a speculative ripple about his control of various companies, including the Graves roads.) Hill neglected to tell the NP's president of his purchase, so that Elliott, sounding alarms, probably never understood Hill's complacency toward Graves's invasion of the Palouse.[22]

With an infusion of Hill money to keep him going, Graves contracted with E. H. Rollins and Sons, one of the investment houses that handled bonds of the subsumed Spokane & Inland, to market a new $2,743,000 issue of first and refunding mortgage bonds. Roughly 46 percent of this issue would be held in escrow by the First Trust and Savings, as trustee, to retire the bonds of the merged companies, and $980,000 to build a hydroelectric generating plant for the railroad at Nine Mile Bridge on the Spokane River. In its prospectus, Rollins called the new issue "an investment of unusual merit," appending an optimistic letter from Graves describing the consolidated Spokane & Inland Empire Railroad Company.[23]

Meanwhile, construction went on. The railroad pushed tracks deeper into the Palouse each month, erected $3,000 depots at Spring Valley, Oakesdale, Palouse City, Rosalia, Thornton, and Colfax, and began freight service as soon as rails were in place. By the end of 1906, lines reached Colfax and Palouse City while the company negotiated for right-of-way into Moscow.

Graves's railroad bought the pyramid of the Palouse, Steptoe Butte, and his Railway Land and Improvement Company, acquiring 644 acres from farmers around it, proposed a townsite at the base and a resort at the top where Cashup Davis's old observatory lay in ruins. At Valleyford, the company graded streets and laid sidewalks, and in Spokane, it built a $110,000 passenger terminal, with golden oak and local marble interior, north across Main Avenue from the site of a new federal court and post-office building. Now all of Graves's street and interurban railways ran to the terminal, and the railroad moved its offices there in April 1906.[24]

When Benjamin Weeks, who had been manager of the Spokane & Inland Empire, took another post in California, Clyde Graves was elevated to general manager, and a short time later, Aubrey White joined the board.

As his lengthening tracks glistened across the Palouse hills, Graves moved to make his railroad independent of Washington Water Power, which sold it a minimum of 3,800 horsepower a year. For a time, he thought to force WWP into a merger. He sketched out this notion for Hill, suggesting that Baker of the First National "could perhaps help us" in negotiations with William Augustus White, the Brooklyn investment broker who virtually controlled Washington Water Power.[25]

In mid-1906 Graves started to build his own generating plant in the narrow granite canyon of the Spokane River at Nine Mile Bridge. He secured right-of-way for a 60,000-volt transmission

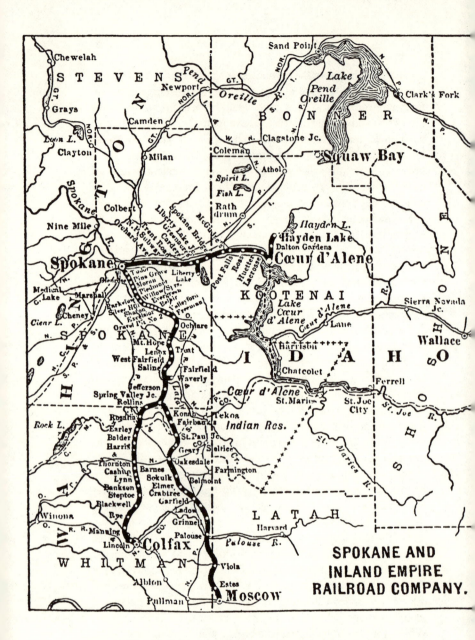

MAP 2. The S&IE produced this map of its system showing the Coeur d'Alene division running eastward to lakes and the Palouse division, south to Spring Valley where it divided into a Moscow and a Colfax division.

line to a Spokane substation; he had earlier obtained a franchise to provide the City of Spokane with electricity and lighting. The New York engineering firm Sanderson and Porter designed and built the 20,000-horsepower Nine Mile plant, setting the powerhouse in the deepest part of the site, as a wing of the dam, where the river made a natural tailrace. When Nine Mile's turbines whirled in 1909, Graves bid to sell surplus power to towns along the railroad and to the Inland Empire Paper mill at Millwood, east of Spokane. (He and William Cowles were among the initial investors in the mill.) Nine Mile Dam created a four-mile reservoir on the Spokane, and a workers' village grew up around the plant.[26]

Graves controlled two other potential power sites: a 152-acre landmark on the Spokane known as the Bowl and Pitcher for its rock formations, and Kettle Falls on the Columbia, where he purchased 450 acres in March 1906 for $77,000 in the name of Granby. Kettle Falls, Graves's largest site, might generate 100,000 horsepower. The Bowl and Pitcher, rated at 25,000 horsepower, had been picked up from the Northern Pacific for $320 by Frank Hogan, who sold it to the Spokane & Inland Empire for $50,000. As time passed, neither site was developed. Grand Coulee Dam eventually flooded Kettle Falls, and the state purchased the Bowl and Pitcher for parkland.[27]

Graves's railroad was now up and running over virtually its entire system (and on the way to Moscow), but revenues were disappointing. Net profits from Coeur d'Alene division and traction lines did not, as forecast, pay interest on the bonds of the whole system. Graves continued to scratch for loans and stock sales to maintain cash flow.

What should have been a banner inaugural year for the Spokane & Inland Empire system soured with the onset of a national depression in the spring of 1907. Northwest bankers growled that this was "a rich man's panic in Wall Street," but Western business shriveled. Banks and commercial houses honored scrip and clearinghouse certificates as money until the panic eased. A story persists that Graves, unable to pay his bills, went to Jim Hill for help and that Hill wrote him a check for $100,000, warning that he could not cash it but could show it to bankers to establish a credit line. Work on the railroad to Moscow had to be suspended for six months; the track was finally completed—behind schedule—on September 15, 1908.

In his annual report (for the fiscal year ending June 30, 1908), Graves observed that "the country has passed through a very trying time, and your property has been more or less affected by the curtailing of business and the difficulty of obtaining necessary funds," but he took an optimistic tone: two units were operating at Nine Mile; Traction division receipts were up 38.3 percent and Coeur d'Alene, 12.4 percent—"exceptional, in view of the fact that the lumber and mining interests in the Coeur d'Alene country were very badly affected by the panic"; and he expected that "the earnings of the company will warrant the resumption of dividends on the preferred rights during the year 1909." The S&IE had paid four dividends of $1.25 each on preferred rights during 1907, all apparently from borrowed funds. The net operating earnings for fiscal 1908, amounting to $310,629, would not pay the interest on its debts.[28]

Graves did not dwell on what his report called "the difficulty of obtaining necessary funds," but he was spending hand-to-mouth as usual: $500,000 in May secured by depositing 6,250 preferred rights (perhaps again to Hill), a loan in June of $200,000 from an unspecified source, $50,000 from the Eastern Townships Bank in August with $10,000 more in September, and sales here and there of preferred rights to people Graves identified for his board as "New York friends." At one point in 1907, the railroad had cut wages 10 percent; it also offered employees a special stock-purchase plan—pennies wherever they could be found to keep the road running.[29]

Despite short funds, the railroad built extensions to Vera and Opportunity, irrigated developments in the Spokane valley. When the line reached Vera, developers sold thirty-eight tracts in one day, and the farmers union put on a barbecue. At Pullman, however, subscribers withdrew their pledges of subsidy because the line did not hold to its construction schedule. Graves himself took off a few weeks with eye trouble. Floods early in 1909 washed out sections of track—money had to be spent for repairs. All in all, the eighteen months after the railroad reached Colfax and Palouse had been precarious days at the slippery brink of disaster.

In their sober reflections, Graves and his closest friends must have realized that the Spokane & Inland Empire was never going to pay. Late in 1908, Graves somberly concluded that the railroad must sell all its remaining preferred rights from the treasury to raise money. He had secured a new loan of $250,000, but that was not going to be enough; the company got some money from promissory notes to the Title Guarantee and Trust Company, New York, which held the Coeur d'Alene division's bonds, and gave an option to Robert Strahorn's secretive North Coast Railroad on real estate and easements for $218,999. Perhaps because he could see no end to indebtedness, one of the original investors, F. Lewis Clark, resigned. Grinnell took his place on the board.[30]

If Graves's company was beginning to unravel, Elliott failed to see the telltale threads. He sent a cross letter to the second vice-president Aubrey White: "I see no reason why you could not give us some of your local Spokane business. . . . When you go down into the Palouse country or to Lake Coeur d'Alene, you are in competition with us."[31]

Neither did patrons of the railroad see its plight. For them, the electric's frequent, rapid service was wondrous and enlivening; it expanded their lives and gave them mobility. The railroad sped country customers to the city in gay spirits on shopping tours, where they thronged stores, restaurants, and theaters. A salesman who once visited two towns in a day now might canvass four or five. City wholesalers delivered orders in one day. Moscow was only three and one-half hours from Spokane; Vera, forty-five minutes, with stops every half mile through the valley.

Patrons rested in comfortable stations, with separate men's and ladies' waiting rooms, listening for the hum or whistle of the oncoming train; they mounted to clean cars with plush or wicker seats and carpeted floors and stained glass windows that reduced sun glare, and they sped across a countryside growing familiar with frequent travel.

The Spokane & Inland Empire promoted excursions to the lakes with hourly runs to Lake Coeur d'Alene and eleven trains a day to Liberty. The farmer's wife shopped in Spokane and reached home in time to ready supper, bubbling with her urban adventures. Clyde Graves wrote memos telling his employees to be courteous. For farm families, the railroad erected sheds at trackside where the men tethered horses while they went to Spokane, installed water in pens for animals awaiting shipment, and like other railroads ran instructional trains with lecturers from the colleges.

All but excursion trains carried both passengers and freight. The Spokane & Inland Empire's freight revenue, remarked a trade journal, was "far greater in proportion to its total gross earnings than most properties," a little more than one-fourth of its income—lumber, farm products, cattle and similar consignments heading into the city and machinery, foods, clothing, and manufactured items carried to country buyers. One of its principal sources of revenue was lumber from the Potlatch company, hauled to a connection with Corbin's Spokane International and thence to the Canadian Pacific. For the people who lived in its service area, the railroad was a boon, and they waved from fields and towns in friendship for the passing red cars.[32]

In holiday spirits, crowds jammed special trains to Coeur d'Alene during the last weeks of July 1909 to register for Indian lands opening on the Coeur d'Alene, Spokane, and Flathead reservations. Police controlled lively throngs at railroad depots and registration offices. On the last day of July, at Gibbs station, a mile and a half west of Coeur d'Alene, the motorman of a special failed to wait for the oncoming regular train and pulled onto the single track. Regular and special smashed head on.

As they rounded a curve moments before the collision, crews and passengers on each train could see oncoming cars speeding toward them; the motorman of the special threw his engine into reverse, virtually stopping it before the impact; at the last instant, the motorman of the regular leaped from his cab. Brakes screeched. Sparks erupted from locked wheels. Some passengers near doorways instinctively hurled themselves from cars. Steel and wood smashed and crumpled. The smoking car telescoped and splintered. Silence for a moment. Then agonized cries of the hurt, the smashing of men breaking themselves free of the crushed cars. Seventeen died, and more than two hundred were injured.[33]

Graves was convalescing at his Hayden Lake home from one of his periodic bouts with "typhoid fever." He immediately ordered an inquiry into the cause of the accident. Tragedy that it was, the Gibbs wreck afforded Graves's admirers a plausible explanation for the waning of his railroad. The *Spokesman-Review* editorially expressed "universal regret that so shocking an experience should befall Mr. Graves and his associates who have built up this great system." Thus, an impression lingers that the Gibbs wreck ruined the railroad. Not true. The railroad's chief executive, Graves, had spent continuously and somewhat extravagantly—only the best for him—throughout its construction, and the revenue could not recoup the costs.

A number of lawsuits asked damages, including one by the motorman of the errant westbound special. Settlements eventually cost the railroad approximately $270,000, a substantial sum paid out gradually but hardly an amount to destroy a railroad of $24 million book value. To his stockholders, Graves reported in 1909, "The deplorable accident... will eat up our earnings for the greater portion of the year, and, much as we regret it, the payment of dividends will be postponed until next year." The operating summary for fiscal 1909 showed increases in passenger and freight revenue, also in Traction Company income.[34]

Before compiling this annual report, however, Graves had begun bargaining to sell the Spokane & Inland Empire. He was not a man for whispering confidences, but those closest to him had an inkling of his purpose when he bought up common stock to deliver a voting majority to a buyer. Most of this stock doubtless came from friends (who also saw that the time had come to get out)—perhaps Clark's 2,349 shares tendered after he resigned and 1,425 from Grinnell, for examples. Graves had about 20,000 common himself. He plainly could not enter the market openly without inflating the price, but as he bought quietly, common rose from $40 to nearly $65 a share, perhaps reflecting the willingness of Graves's buyer to pay, and Graves apparently sold the stock at about $74. At that price, Graves, who originally put in $40,000, realized $1,480,000.[35]

James J. Hill, of course, was the predictable buyer. He already held 21,000 shares. Through the Northwestern Improvement Company, a Northern Pacific subsidiary familiar in the Palouse as a railroad land agency, Hill acquired 39,000 more, which gave him 60 percent of the common. He divided capital stock on paper between the Great Northern and the Northern Pacific, $3,465,300 to the GN and $100 less to the NP. (Recall that as a result of J. P. Morgan's reorganization of the Northern Pacific in the late nineties, Hill directed affairs of the NP as well as the GN.)

When newspapers learned of the sale on October 28, 1909, they reported that Hill bought the Graves road to keep it away from the Chicago, Milwaukee & St. Paul. In retrospect, this does not seem credible, for, as the *Spokesman-Review* observed, "Hill and Graves interests together are stated to have always held control" of the road. Moreover, Hill was involved in Granby. Graves could not have afforded to double-cross him by dealing with the Milwaukee.[36]

Some minority stockholders, surprised by the sale, reacted with anger, charging that Graves "sold them out"; but the *Spokesman-Review* regretted Graves's "withdrawal." With him in charge, "the extension of the system and development of the country tributary to Spokane were inseparable," the editor wrote. "Mr. Graves has done a great deal for this city and for the Inland Empire."[37]

Ten years later, however, when the Spokane & Inland Empire went into receivership, the Spokane periodical *Mining Truth* published an acidic editorial declaring the railroad's liquidation "the worst financial blow ever suffered by this city. . . . It was essentially the promotion of certain banking interests—safe and sane advisers, who cheerfully extracted the public savings and then 'stepped from under' with one unanimous movement. . . . It has done more harm than all the mining promotions of twenty years, and we are quite sure that ours will be the only voice to protest." The Spokane & Inland Empire fiasco, concluded *Mining Truth*, was proof that "all rottenness is not confined to mining promotion."[38]

At Hill's invitation, Graves stayed on as president of the Spokane & Inland Empire at a salary of $10,000 a year (he had been donating his services) with a new loan of $300,000 for construction in progress. He bubbled with plans: extend Traction routes, connect Colfax and Pullman with a line, electrify the Northern Pacific to Moscow, build a spur to Post Falls flour and saw mills and another from the East Broadway streetcar line to Stanton's meat-packing plant, which was being enlarged with a view to setting up a string of smaller packinghouses throughout the Palouse country.

To Graves's proposals for spurs, Elliott growled: "It hardly seems necessary . . . to spend money to take business away from the Northern Pacific." His letters changed from comradely to pessimistic. In December, Elliott wrote Graves that he and Hill agreed that all the plans ought to wait, and he directed Clyde Graves "to prune expenses to the lowest possible notch" in order to pay something on the bonds and floating debt.[39]

The Northern Pacific directors chafed that a railroad they controlled had to honor Graves's competing traffic agreements with the Canadian Pacific and the Milwaukee while a new rival crept upon them—the automobile. These were the final days of large projects in transcontinental rail construction for the Northwest. The automobile flood began as a trickle: mounted high for rutted, bumpy country wagon roads, autos promised adventure; they elbowed aside railroads for short runs and pleasure drives. Accustomed to gasoline engines, farmers quickly took to autos. The state legislature was already debating road construction for automobiles, and the machines were so numerous by 1910 that Spokane enacted a traffic code. Chambers of commerce set out road signs pointing to their towns. Motor stages preempted the most popular railroad passenger routes in fair weather, and truck owners, bound for town, hauled freight at cut rates rather than drive empty one way. Graves himself had offered prizes of $3,000 for model automobile roads tributary to his electric line, appointing a judging committee of college presidents and a state railroad commission member.

Graves gradually realized that Hill and Elliott had no interest in building up the Spokane & Inland Empire; they saw it as a feeder, to be maintained, and the street railways as a bothersome appendage perhaps salable to Washington Water Power.

Yet, Elliott hesitated to discard Graves. "Jay P. Graves has a great many friends and admirers in Spokane who think the creation of the Spokane Inland Empire by him has meant a great deal to the building up of Spokane," he wrote Carl R. Gray, president of the Spokane, Portland & Seattle, who was about to take command of the Graves system. "Spokane is in some ways a very sensitive town, and it would be easy to set them against us if they think we are taking away too much of the local management of the Inland Road."[40]

But when Clyde Graves, visiting St. Paul, handed Hill and Elliott a list of unpaid bills—$43,000 to Washington Water Power, $84,000 to Westinghouse, $92,000 for paving required by the City of Spokane, and more—they resolved that Jay Graves must go. Louis Hill advised Graves, in a letter so short as to be curt, that the trustees on June 15, 1911, would elect Gray president and C. A. Coolidge, also an SP&S employee, general manager.[41] The new president found the railroad system in a worse tangle than he had anticipated. "It looks to me as if the compilation of statistics has been turned over to some person with instructions to prepare them with a certain purpose in view," he wrote Elliott, "that purpose being to deceive." He went promptly to Washington Water Power to inquire whether it might buy the traction lines and cancel its contract to supply power to the Spokane & Inland Empire.[42]

Gray would be the first of four presidents of the Spokane &

Inland Empire under its new owners; the others, also presidents of the SP&S, were John Young, 1913–15, L. C. Gilman, 1915–18, and Frank Elliott, 1918–19. None could make it profitable. "It is not an easy matter to make both ends meet on the Inland," Gilman reported to an NP vice-president. "In a country like the Palouse, every farmer has an automobile. . . . I can see nothing to do for the present, except to hold the property together, earn as much and spend as little as possible."[43]

The Great Northern and Northern Pacific had periodically lent the Spokane & Inland Empire money to pay interest on its bonds, but by 1918 they were estimating the junk value of the electric system. They were not encouraged by a national report showing that, despite swollen war shipments and higher rates, the net incomes of American electric railroads fell 82.16 percent between 1917 and 1918. Influenza kept people home, strikes crippled the Northwest lumber industry, railcar shortages imposed embargoes, and autos multiplied like rabbits, all cutting into revenue. The Great Northern and Northern Pacific managers concluded there was no reason to go on—they refused to pay bond interest or sinking funds. The officers of the Spokane & Inland Empire, said Frank Elliott, had decided to "let things drift until January 1st [1918], upon which date it is understood the bondholders will commence foreclosure proceedings and ask for the appointment of a receiver."[44]

The decision to abandon the Spokane & Inland Empire stirred galling memories, as J. M. Hannaford, now president of the Northern Pacific, observed: "I have tried . . . to get our Executive Committee to put this whole matter of the Spokane and Inland into a committee's hands that could grasp the complicated financial situation that was worked up by Mr. Graves and the late Mr. [James] Hill. . . . The Northern Pacific has its own lines into the very best of this territory and I do not think should have become a partner in this unloading by Mr. Graves and his associates."[45]

Finally, on petition of the First Trust and Savings, trustee for a thousand or more bondholders in every state in the U.S. and in Europe, a receiver took over the Spokane & Inland Empire on January 9, 1919. In thirteen years, it had paid four dividends on preferred rights, nothing on common stock, and retired but $348,000 of $4 million in bonds. The following November, E. H. Rollins and Sons, also representing bondholders, acquired the railroad for $3.6 million at a receiver's sale. The Spokane & Inland

Empire, which had had so many names that few ever called it by the right one, now was reorganized into two, the Spokane & Eastern Railway & Power Company to manage Nine Mile and the Coeur d'Alene branch, and the Inland Empire Railway to operate the Palouse lines. As its service deteriorated, Spokane & Eastern sold off power plant, streetcar lines, resorts, real estate, and other assets, until 1927 when the Great Northern again took the line and changed its name to the Spokane, Coeur d'Alene & Palouse, and then to the Spokane & Idaho Northern.[46]

The Spokane terminal was sold in 1930 for a Sears, Roebuck store site—which has since become the Spokane Public Library—and trains were rerouted to the Great Northern depot. The terminal, on filled ground, had cracked walls and its foundation had begun to crumble.

The electric railroad died by snippets. Washington Water Power bought the Hayden Lake distribution system in 1930 and ended electric train service there. The last electric passenger trains sang over the rails to Moscow on April 1, 1939; the last passenger run to Coeur d'Alene took place in July 1940. For perhaps thirty years after, the Great Northern used segments of the line for freight with diesel engines. As late as the 1980s, Burlington Northern served a grain elevator at Viola, Idaho, with a portion of the old track. That Jay Graves's route remained useful for so long confirms the accuracy of his vision. But the electric railroad finally expired, leaving empty track, abandoned cuts in Palouse hills, deserted stations, and the rancor of those who had invested in an effervescent dream in a vanished era.[47]

CHAPTER 5

Granby

While Jay Graves built the Spokane & Inland Empire and plotted Spokane real estate strategy, he remained vice-president and general manager of the Granby Consolidated Mining, Smelting and Power Company, Ltd. He had barely missed connections with James Hill's man for funds to attempt a raid for stock control of Granby and had stood by in 1902 while the large block of stock he wanted went instead to a syndicate formed by William H. Nichols.

A manufacturing chemist from New York, Nichols at fifty was a transcendent figure in the copper industry of the United States. With such men as John Stanton, the industry's grand old man and statistician, and Boston financiers, Nichols held the center of the copper business; he was one of those who manipulated supply and price and one who joined other princes of copper to destroy Amalgamated Copper.[1]

Nichols and friends apparently bought Granby stock on the basis that Graves had offered it to Hill, four dollars a share.

Four members of the Nichols syndicate were elected directors at Granby's annual meeting in Montreal in 1903: Nichols, Stanton, Jacob Langeloth, president of American Metal (a smelterer and marketer), and young Clement S. Houghton, a wealthy Boston investor. Both Nichols and Langeloth were familiar with Granby's product, and they also relied on a detailed analysis that a noted geologist, Otto Sussman, completed for Nichols. With Sussman's report in hand, five of Nichols's people ventured into the wilds of Grand Forks, British Columbia, to see Granby for themselves a month before the meeting: Stanton; George M. Luther, manager, and J. B. F. Hereshoff, vice-president, Nichols Chemical; Houghton; and William A. Paine, senior partner of Paine Webber and Company, Boston investment bankers with extensive copper and railroad interests. They toured the claims, the mines, and the smelter with Stephen Miner (still president), Graves, Aubrey White, Hodges, and Flumerfelt, and to a man, they gave enthusiastic interviews. Stanton, a lively seventy-four, told a reporter, "I must admit I came West prepared to discount a great deal of what I had heard.... Nowhere have I seen superior methods." Hereshoff observed that the mines were a "magnificent, monotonous mass of homogenous ore."[2]

Graves now fell under the direction of some of the most capable men in the copper industry. They urged him to pay a dividend and to step up development work to find out how much ore might actually be in the Phoenix claims. With a dividend, its debts paid, Granby would close out its "transitional period" from prospects to producing mines, the Boston News Bureau commented, and could list its stock for trading on the Boston exchange.[3]

Oddly, considering that able copper men invested perhaps two million in Granby, nobody knew the size of its ore reserves. They were considered huge, and it is common in mining to develop reserves incrementally, adding new as known ores are removed. "Up to about 1904 it would have been impossible to figure actual tons in sight," explained a superintendent. As they learned more precisely the extent of ore bodies at Phoenix, Granby's new directors bought surrounding claims until, in six years, they expanded their ground from 11 to 35 claims and fractions.[4]

Granby and other smelters of interior British Columbia relied for coke on the Crow's Nest Pass Coal Company, Ltd., organized in 1897 by Toronto investors to exploit coal deposits on the western slope of the mountains that divide British Columbia from Alberta. The directors and the president, George S. Cox, also president of the Canada Life Assurance Company, left operations to G. G. S. Lindsey, whom the CPR president, Shaughnessy, regarded as "oily and adroit." James Hill thought Crow's Nest "coal and coke . . . of a superior quality" but grumbled that the directors were men "inclined to speculate" who held the company's business at arm's length, "more as a stock exchange matter than a coal mine." Carelessly managed, unaggressive, Crow's Nest seemed content to rake in dividends from its monopoly of the coal and coke trade of the interior.[5]

Graves, the British Columbia Copper Company, and even Walter Aldridge at Trail tried to apply pressure to manage efficiently on Cox's company through the Canadian Pacific. Shaughnessy, himself nonplussed by Cox's casual view of the coal business, politely hedged. "If I can do anything to help your company secure the requisite supply of coal, I shall be glad to do so," he wrote Graves, but added candidly, "The Crow's Nest Company, however, appear to be quite unequal to the demands." Shaughnessy set out to blunt the Crow's Nest monopoly: his railroad prospected for coal, "not so much [for] the mining . . . as the desire to keep a proper check on the Crow's Nest Company with reference to quantity, quality and price for Canadian consumers." If a tariff compact could be made with the United States, Shaughnessy thought Crow's Nest could sell coal to much of the American West.[6]

Hill also had difficulty getting enough coal for his railroad. He took a direct approach to the problem; he bought a substantial stock interest in the Crow's Nest Company, and thereafter he offered a good deal of unsolicited advice to Cox and Lindsey on managing it. He completed the first section of his own railroad into the Crow's Nest coal district in 1901 between Morrissey, B.C., a shipping station, and Jennings, Montana, on the Great Northern main line.[7]

Hill's entry in the Crow's Nest did not improve coke deliveries to Granby. But prospectors had staked bituminous coal claims north of Grand Forks on the west fork of the north fork of the Kettle River, and soon five Spokane men organized the International Coal and Coke Company, a Washington corporation, to open the deposits.

The principal in this company, E. J. Dyer, president of the Exchange National Bank of Spokane, had done business with Graves for years. Either Graves put Dyer up to forming the company or Dyer tipped off Graves to the coal discovery. As usual, Graves sent the Spokane mining engineer Nelson Linsley to look and, based on his "extremely cursory" inspection, bonded fifteen coal claims for Granby.

Graves installed Flumerfelt as president, H. N. Galer as vice-president, and his brother Will Graves as secretary of International Coal and Coke Company, and he bought nine veins at Blairmore, Alberta, on the line of the Crow's Nest Pass railway.[8]

Meanwhile, Jim Hill came to Grand Forks, and many Canadians hoped that his presence would hurry the Canadian Pacific construction across the southern reaches of the province. For a time, Shaughnessy used the courts to hamper Hill but eventually advised his agent in Vancouver that "the chief solicitor is of the opinion that the Vancouver Eastern has a legal right to complete its line." Of some Canadians who applauded Hill, however, Shaughnessy predicted darkly, "These British Columbia gentlemen may begin to realize, when it is too late, that, in their efforts to provide competition with the C.P.R., they have been giving the Province a distinct and serious set-back."[9]

Hill's route from Marcus (Bossburg) led up the Kettle River valley to a border crossing south of Christina Lake and thence west to Grand Forks. While he built, he threatened a rate war. In 1902 his Vancouver, Victoria & Eastern reached Grand Forks; with Dominion authority, it crossed the Canadian Pacific tracks to the Granby smelter and commenced hacking a twenty-three-mile line to Phoenix, 2,600 feet higher than Grand Forks. On the last day of 1903, an inspecting engineer approved the Phoenix line for freighting. Because ballasting was not finished and seven of eleven bridges lacked guard rails and bracing, he limited train speed to ten miles an hour. To reach Phoenix, the GN engineers had, in places, adopted 3-percent grades and 16-degree curvatures, creating a steep, twisting mountain railway. Two months after the inspection, with ballasting and bridges done and a "well designed neat station house at Phoenix," the route was opened to public traffic.[10]

At its Phoenix mines, Granby extracted ores from the Knob Hill and Old Ironsides both from glory holes worked by steam shovel and from tunnels connected to the Victoria shaft. Ore came out at the portals of tunnels 2 and 3. Great Northern trains loaded at tunnel 3; both railroads ran spurs to tunnel 2, and the CPR, to the Curlew portal. Each railroad maintained separate tracks and yards at the smelter, connected by crossovers, and together they ran a switch engine to move ores, copper blister, coke, and freight in and out of the plant. By late 1903, Granby had started tunnel 4 with a portal in the town of Phoenix, at the foot of Church Street.

Once the Great Northern (as the VV&E) reached Phoenix, assuring an American route from Grand Forks to New York, William Nichols decisively changed the corporate structure of Granby. He ousted most of the Canadians and put in American directors; in June 1904 he retired Graves's William Yolen Williams to consultant status and appointed A. B. W. Hodges general superintendent reporting independently of Graves to the directors; at the annual meeting that year, Nichols installed Jacob Langeloth as president. All of the Canadian directors resigned (by request) except Robinson of the Eastern Townships Bank.

As the Grand Forks *News-Gazette* observed, "Granby has become

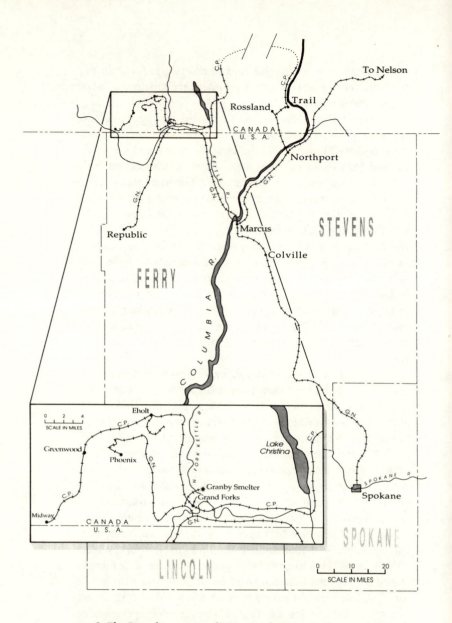

MAP 3. The Boundary mining district in relation to Spokane and the railroads serving it. The inset shows locations of towns but the rail routes are imprecise, indicative rather than accurate. (*By David Anderson, Eastern Washington University*)

an American company." Stephen Miner protested to reporters that he was still "one of the largest stockholders," but he was now small fry. Graves continued to hold the titles of vice-president and general manager. The roster of new directors suggests, however, that his position depended on the sanction of James J. Hill.[11]

The board elected in October 1904 consisted of Nichols, John Stanton, Langeloth, George Luther, Graves, and Robinson, continuing directors; and George F. Baker, Jr., of the First National Bank, New York; Payne Whitney, scion of the New York Whitneys; George C. Clark of Clark, Dodge and Company, New York investment bankers; Henry Lee Higginson, Boston banker; and Arthur C. James of Phelps, Dodge and Company—a glittering assemblage of the American copper industry's leading technicians and financiers. Baker represented Hill. As long as Baker was a director, Granby periodically had to deny that Hill was in charge. Baker's presence showed that Hill had listened to Graves during those cozy conversations behind closed doors in his red sandstone mansion on Summit Avenue overlooking St. Paul and the Mississippi.[12]

The new lineup lent credence to rumors Shaughnessy heard of a "secret compact that is alleged to exist between the Great Northern interests and the Granby smelter people." The provincial minister of mines observed that, for the first time, Granby superintendents and managers "seem loth to furnish suitable information" for his yearly report, adding that the directorate appeared to have undergone a complete change.[13]

Hill's bold penetration of Canadian Pacific demesne dismayed Shaughnessy. Consequently, when George Turner, former U.S. Senator, approached Shaughnessy for a branch to his Sullivan mine and smelter at Kimberley, B.C., the Canadian Pacific president enlisted Turner to form a Washington company to build a railroad from Canada to Spokane and Seattle, suggesting D. C. Corbin as promoter. Negotiations went on for two years in difficult times—"at the moment," Shaughnessy said in October 1903, "there are no purchasers for even the most gilt-edged securities"—until Corbin, shooing Turner away to his duties on the Alaskan Boundary Tribunal, at last organized a company of old friends, backers of the Spokane Falls & Northern.

Corbin built the Spokane International north from Spokane through the Idaho panhandle to a junction with the Canadian Pacific at Eastport. The railroad gave the Inland Empire connections to the Midwest independent of the GN and the NP. The CPR held an option on 52 percent of the capital stock (which it exercised in 1916) and helped sell bonds, pushing off some on the Soo Line. "Our arrangement with Mr. Corbin is really in the nature of a traffic agreement," Shaughnessy explained to the Canadian minister of justice, "on a basis that should make the line . . . profitable." The Spokane International opened for business on November 1, 1906. The industry magazine *Railway Age* cackled that "the Canadian Pacific has struck the Great Northern a body blow in the war of territorial aggression between these mighty railway builders" with a route through "a region hitherto controlled by the Great Northern." On July 1, 1907, the Canadian Pacific inaugurated deluxe service between St. Paul and Spokane, 784 miles in Canada and 700 in the U.S., and the Soo published schedules for Portland and San Francisco by connection with the Union Pacific at Spokane.[14]

But the Canadian Pacific had not struck a body blow in Boundary country. Shaughnessy cut "to the lowest possible rate . . . that will yield a living profit," but Hill at first hauled Granby consignments at cost. Consequently, the Great Northern between 1904 and 1910 would carry three-fifths of the freight of Boundary and 68 percent of Granby's. Hill raised rates as traffic increased.[15]

At the end of September 1905, Hill himself, a thick-set, plain man, came with friends in a seven-car special train for his second look—he had visited in 1902—at Grand Forks and Phoenix. In Hill's party, an editor picked out Whitney, clean shaven and athletic, Baker, tall, whiskered, white-haired, and "outdoorsy," and Graves, lean and solicitous. Hunching against a rainstorm, they spent an hour touring the smelter and a few minutes watching a steam shovel gnaw at Phoenix.[16]

Graves had squeezed out the dividend in 1903 that Nichols demanded, Granby's first, an unimpressive $133,630, but a promise, at any rate, that there would be more in the future. With Nichols as goad and the Great Northern at hand, Granby now embarked on a substantial enlargement of mines and smelter and a policy of regular dividends. The company had dug 290,000 tons of ore in 1903; with Nichols pushing, it extracted 514,000 in 1904 and 551,304 in 1905, and it would continue to increase its yield almost every year.[17]

The smelter added two furnaces as the Great Northern built toward Grand Forks; in 1905, two more, and after that, it twice enlarged all eight furnaces to a capacity of 4,000 to 4,500 tons a day. Matte was converted in thirteen shells to 100,000 pounds of blister daily, 98.5 percent copper, and cast into 220-pound bars for shipment to New York refineries. Granby also recovered other mineral values in processing, sometimes as much as 300,000 ounces of silver and 40,000 of gold in a year.[18]

No other mining enterprise in Boundary rivaled Granby. And without most of Granby's business, the Canadian Pacific lost money on its service there. "We have not been receiving adequate returns on the investment . . . that we made for the purpose of opening up several [Boundary] mining districts," Shaughnessy grumbled. British Columbia Copper, the second most productive company, with its Mother Lode mine and smelter at Greenwood, belonged to a New York syndicate headed by Colgate Hoyt, a Baptist friend of John D. Rockefeller.

During the life of the Boundary district, there were said to be seventy-seven producing mines, some flaring and some flickering out like candles in a wind.

Granby's expansion took place during a swell of rising copper prices, perhaps manipulated. Between 1904 and 1907, copper prices at New York doubled from twelve to twenty-five cents a pound, spurred by a burgeoning electrical industry and demand from the Orient—China gearing up under its dowager empress to copy the West and Japan warring with Russia and then rebuilding. Even though Arizona, Utah, Nevada, and New Mexico poured copper into the marketplace, the price went up. There were rumors of collusion among processors. (The Federal Trade Commission concluded that allegations of collusion were probably true.) If Granby could profit at twelve cents, as Albert Ledoux had estimated in 1902, this was prosperity indeed, with an average price for Granby blister of 13.33 cents.[19]

Granby converted its capital stock on December 1, 1905, from 1,500,000 shares at $10 par to 150,000 at $100 par (140,297 issued) and redistributed shares on the basis of one new for ten old. The conversion pushed up the market price per share and drove out small investors, solidifying the voting predominance of the majority owners. The asking price at Boston inflated to $45 and went as high as $82, and when the New York Stock Exchange allowed copper listings, Granby was admitted to trading there on January 23, 1907. (For one heady moment, it would reach $135.)[20]

In terms of world trade, Granby was a pebble on the beach. In these years, Canada mined no more than 3 to 4 percent of the copper sold. But Granby towered in Boundary: it employed hundreds in mines and smelter and created jobs for other hundreds in the towns, on the railroads, and in the coalfields; it was, for a time, the largest copper smelter in the British Empire and second in the world only to the Washoe works at Anaconda, Montana. By 1906, Boundary mines had produced an estimated thirty million dollars' worth of copper, gold, and silver, nearly three-fourths of it from Granby.

The one sour note in Granby's symphony of success sounded from Crow's Nest, which never achieved a reliable schedule of coke deliveries. Shortages of coke forced unexpected shutdowns. Langeloth and Graves fumed. They could, they assured Hill, double production if they could get enough coke.

The Crow's Nest Company had offered stock to Granby, presumably to admit Granby to its management, but at the time Graves and Langeloth "were not able to see any advantage to them in acquiring shares" and instead signed "a long date contract for coke." Indeed, Crow's Nest's once exclusive syndicate of Toronto men now seemed eager for new money, and Jim Hill discovered why: the company was paying dividends not earned. Hill saw an opportunity for control; he dispatched Graves to buy more Crow's Nest. Graves apparently went to C. E. Gault, who had been in the original Granby company, for 3,000 shares for Granby, and bought 25 elsewhere for himself, giving Hill, Granby, and Graves among them 52 percent. Hill remarked to Graves, "Later on you should take a place on the board," and Graves did, as Hill put his own people in place.[21]

Graves, usually chatty with newspapermen, would not talk about Crow's Nest. A reporter who inquired got only: "Sometimes we do foolish things. As we get older, we do them more often." Even though they now owned the company, Graves and Granby could not wring enough coke from Crow's Nest. "Graves is thoroughly convinced that there is nothing to hope for from the present management," Hill warned Cox, still president. Yet the Crow's Nest Company increased coal production 21 percent, and coke, 7.5 percent in 1907, a year marked by labor strife. Granby and other smelters closed with falling copper prices and strikes for higher wages.[22]

Granby's crews voted on Christmas Day to accept lower pay and forgo recognition of the Western Federation of Miners. Its managers ignored the union. "I always talk to union committees," Hodges, Granby Superintendent, observed, but he paid no heed to their requests. Involved in a strike, the manager of British Columbia Copper complained it was "useless to expect any cooperation from The Granby Company. They have always put it up to us to pull their chesnuts [sic] from the fire" in district-wide labor disputes.[23]

Ominous news, meanwhile, came from Phoenix: drilling crews had struck barren rock. The copper deposits were bottoming out. The tidings brought Graves to Phoenix by automobile to inspect the mines with Hodges. The city brass band serenaded the visitor at the Granby office, and he gave the players twenty dollars. Graves had been an absentee manager for some time; he was busy with his Spokane & Inland Empire and real estate, and he and Amanda had taken to motoring south in their White steamer to winter in Pasadena, California, usually at The Maryland.

Graves and Hodges looked for new properties (and Hodges, it would seem, cast about quietly for a new job). That genial Welshman, William Yolen Williams, had been scouting mining claims for four years, ranging from Alaska to Oregon, and now he offered three: Hidden Creek, Chelan, and Flin Flon, "three of the nicest claims that ever delighted an engineer." Of these, Granby's board chose Hidden Creek, nine claims about twenty miles from the Alaska–British Columbia border in a sea-level valley ringed by glaciers. Seagoing vessels—the only transportation—reached Hidden Creek through Hastings Arm of Observatory Inlet, a strait between steep, rocky timbered shores about 90 miles from Prince Rupert and more than 550 north of Vancouver. The claims were said to have been worked by Indians before they were staked in 1899 by a prospector who sold for $6,000 to M. K. Rodgers, a Denver mining man who represented Marcus Daly.

The Daly estate's managers let Hidden Creek go. Williams had visited the place three or four times. On his recommendation, Granby bought 80 percent from Rodgers for $400,000, a price Rodgers called "shockingly inadequate." Rodgers kept 20 percent, thus insinuating himself into Granby and eventually onto the board.[24]

That Hidden Creek would make a mine seemed certain. On a hurried inspection, Graves found that earlier owners had trenched and tunneled into two bodies of mixed pyrite and chalcopyrite, one 4 to 6 percent copper, the other, 4.5 to 5 percent, with more iron than silica, a balance desirable for smelting. Preliminary diamond drilling indicated an initial 4 million tons of ore with much of the property remaining to be examined. A waterfall would generate electricity; Granby Bay was deep enough for ocean vessels; the climate was mild—an average temperature ranging from 24 degrees Fahrenheit in January to 58 degrees in July and August—for year-round shipping. Hodges chose this time to resign for a position in Peru. To make an orderly transition to a new manager, the company sent the geologist Otto Sussman to Phoenix for a routine inspection. The directors were predictably stunned by Sussman's estimate that Phoenix would exhaust its ores in less than five years. In ugly exchanges behind closed doors, Langeloth accused Hodges of "stripping" the mines.

For Hodges, leaving Granby ended a comfortable tenure; he was a personage in Grand Forks, a musician for town dances, the owner of 200 feet of waterfront, a cabin, and launch at Lake Christina; his two daughters, schooled in Spokane, had married in his home. Forty Grand Forks businessmen paid him their respects at a farewell banquet. After toasting king, Hodges, the province, and the mining and smelting industry, they presented Hodges with a gold watch and his wife with a diamond ring. Langeloth telegraphed regrets.

Unluckily, intimations that Phoenix was bottoming slipped out with Hodges's departure. A storm broke over Granby; its stock plunged as ominous rumors spread; Hodges, they said, had resigned knowing the end was near. The *Canadian Mining Journal* declared, "The public has a right to know whether stupidity or something less excusable has brought about the present unfortunate circumstances." Graves, roused by telegrams to Pasadena, claimed that he "had not visited the mine personally for about 18 months."[25]

The reputations of its directors buoyed Granby against a blow that might have ruined a lesser company, for, as the *Engineering and Mining Journal* said, "No one will believe . . . that such men as Higginson, James, Langeloth and Nichols, besides others on this board, have intentionally lent themselves to any deception." But the magazine added ruefully, "No event has done so much to destroy public confidence in mining investments."[26]

Sussman's report, released for stockholders' scrutiny for the first time at the 1910 meeting (and printed in the annual report), estimated the remaining Phoenix reserves at roughly 5.6 million tons that would last "somewhat less than 4½ years." His figures stood in stark contradiction to Hodges's statement in the 1909 report: "Our ore reserves are largely increased and we have ore in sight for many years to come."[27]

At the annual meeting, stockholders demanded to know how the bad news leaked out before they heard it. Langeloth could only respond that no officer or director bought or sold stock on the basis of Sussman's findings, thereby implying that the board had known the situation for months. No one explained, the *Engineering and Mining Journal* commented, "why this mine . . . was suddenly found to be of decidedly limited life." And even though Granby's production and earnings were higher than they had been in 1909, Langeloth refused to declare a dividend. Stung by "criticism to which the management has been subjected," he resigned.[28]

No one mentioned Hidden Creek, although it was poised to gallop to Granby's rescue. Within three weeks of that pothering annual meeting of 1910, Granby bonded Hidden Creek. It would prove to be the mine Granby hoped for. Jay Graves, who had been ill with recurring intestinal infection, sounded out several board members about his resignation in 1911 and offered it formally in 1912—when, perhaps not coincidentally, James Hill "retired" from active railroading. But Nichols and the directors kept Graves on as general manager to see Hidden Creek from development to operation; they gave him an assistant general manager, however, F. M. Sylvester, the engineer who had come out from New York to be on-site manager for construction of the Nine Mile Dam for Graves's Spokane & Inland Empire.

On the slopes beside a deep inlet on Hastings Arm, Granby Bay, workmen erected a company town, Anyox, with barracks for single men, housing for managers and married men, hospital, shops, and warehouse. On a clear day, one could see glaciers glistening above surrounding forests. Along the waterfront, where the tide rose twenty-three feet, they built five hundred-foot wooden wharfs floating parallel with the shore where vessels of the Coastwise Steamship and Barge Company, Seattle, docked at low tide. They dammed Falls Creek with rocks for a power plant that drove compressors to drill the mine tunnels, ran a lumber mill and eventually supplied current for the town and the ore mill. To the mine portals a mile and a half above the town, they laid a plank wagon road and an electric tramway to haul ores to mill and docks. And as miners tunneled deeper, they found larger deposits and richer ore. Hidden Creek, Graves acknowledged, was "bigger and better than we realized." The company enlarged docks and mill and, after shipping concentrates for a year to Grand Forks, built a smelter at Anyox.

By the middle of 1912, Granby was clearly back on its feet. Graves, however, was leaving more and more work to Sylvester. Again citing poor health, he resigned as general manager at the 1913 meeting but held his place on the board as vice-president. Sylvester succeeded him as general manager and was named a director. For Graves, it was a good time to go: that year Granby produced record tonnage, paid $450,000 in dividends, and retained a surplus.[29]

Yet, there was more behind Graves's resignation than poor health. He was making one last appeal to Hill to "figure out some plan by which sufficient shares could be acquired to vest the control with my friends" so that he, Graves, "might be elected president and be a dominating influence in the company." He pointed out that many of Nichols's original buyers had died or sold and that if Hill supported him in stock purchases "by a banking house in a quiet way . . . the shares might be acquired by some gentlemen who would hold them and cooperate with me in the further development of the property." But, for whatever reason, this proposed raid on Granby, like Graves's earlier one, did not come off.[30]

The Anyox smelter blew in during March 1914, treating self-fluxing ores. After a decade, changes in the character of the deposits would require flotation. For coal and coke, Granby opened the Cassidy colliery about eight miles from Nanaimo on Vancouver Island. By 1916, Granby stock again reached $120 on the exchanges, and the company paid its highest dividends. Anyox would produce copper blister until 1935 and then, its six ore bodies nearing exhaustion, would sell to Consolidated Mining and Smelting. World War I demand for copper extended the life of Phoenix: the last carload of ore rattled down the mountain railroad to Grand Forks on June 14, 1919. The old glory holes would be worked periodically thereafter until the end of 1978. By then, the town of Phoenix was rubble—its buildings savaged by scavengers for brick and lumber, second-growth forest creeping over old scars in the

A Great Northern ore train crossing a curved wooden trestle 193 feet high near Phoenix shows the twisting mountain line between Phoenix mines and the Granby smelter at Grand Forks. (Boundary Museum No. 219, Grand Forks, B.C.)

Early building at Phoenix. At the top of First Street, above the emerging town, is the Victoria shaft portal and, at left, a Granby company hotel for mine workers. (Boundary Museum No. 342, Grand Forks, B.C.)

Phoenix in 1909. The principal business street, First, runs uphill to mine portals. At this time, Phoenix was served by two competing railways. Nothing is left of the town today but a monument. (Boundary Museum No. 322, Grand Forks, B.C.)

Great Northern Railway trestle at Deadman's Gulch on the route from Grand Forks to Phoenix, B.C. The structure indicates the difficulty of building a road to the mines at Phoenix. (EWSHS No. 81-441)

Granby smelter under construction on a scooped-out hillside above the town of Grand Forks. The plant ran its first batch of ores on April 11, 1900. (Boundary Museum No. 145, Grand Forks, B.C.)

Stephen H. C. Miner, who joined Graves in seeking Canadian investors in Granby, stands between two unidentified women on the train. William Yolen Williams, mine manager, stands at right with vest unbuttoned. (Boundary Museum No. 211, Grand Forks, B.C.)

Investors who joined William Nichols of New York in Granby came to see the mines. Left to right: Clement Houghton, John Stanton, A. L. White, W. A. Paine, A. B. W. Hodges, George Luther, William Y. Williams, J. B. F. Hereshoff, and J. P. Graves. (Author's collection)

The Palouse dunes required cuts for Graves's electric railroad. Although most of the construction was done with horse-drawn equipment, steam-shovels were brought in for heavy trenching. (EWSHS No. L87-44)

Crews stringing wire for the Palouse lines of the Spokane & Inland Empire Railroad. Pantographs atop the electric locomotives took operating current from overhead wires. (EWSHS)

The hilly Palouse country required fills to build a roadbed of moderate grade. Using horses and fresnoes, crews construct a long fill, circa 1908. (T. B. Keith collection No. 14-64, University of Idaho)

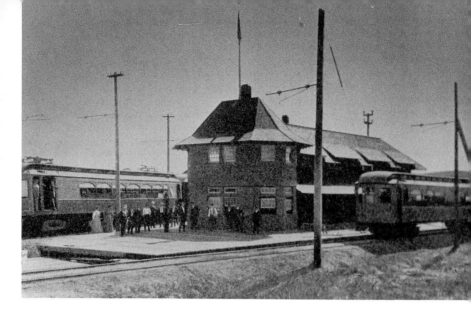

The Spokane & Inland Empire lines from Colfax and Moscow joined at Spring Valley, a town created by the railway. (*Electric Railway Journal*, April 24, 1909, p. 790)

Jay Graves, center on train platform in a gray greatcoat, and other S&IE officers. Immediately to Graves's left is F. A. Blackwell, and to his left, Clyde Graves. F. Lewis Clark stands second from left on platform; Fred Grinnell, center, on track. (EWSHS)

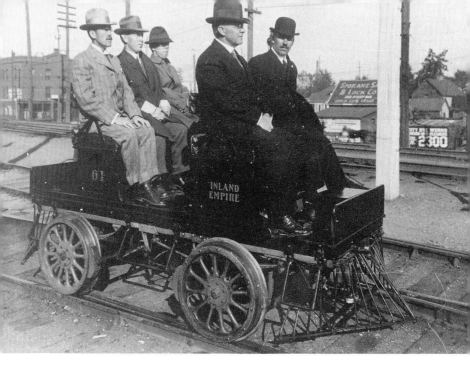

Off to inspect S&IE tracks. Jay Graves, leaning forward in front wearing derby; Clyde Graves, his son and railroad general manager, at his right. Others unidentified. (Author's collection)

Four miles north of Colfax, S&IE drove a 622-foot tunnel to avoid a one-mile detour. The tunnel was the cheaper alternative. (*Spokane's Electric Railroads,* S&IE booklet)

Nine Mile dam and powerhouse on the Spokane River shortly after completion. The powerhouse was placed in the river as a wing of the dam. Graves sold much of the current to other users. (EWSHS)

S&IE Spokane freight terminal. The railroad's freight operations lay between the freight yards of the Great Northern and Northern Pacific, with spurs to both for transfer. (*Railway Age,* Sept. 13, 1907, 354)

S&IE passenger and freight station at Valleyford. Architect Albert Held planned nine S&IE stations on the same general design. (EWSHS No. L86-202)

A crowded platform at the S&IE station at Garfield. The pantograph shows clearly on the passenger locomotive (right) and the station follows the standard design. (Washington State University Library)

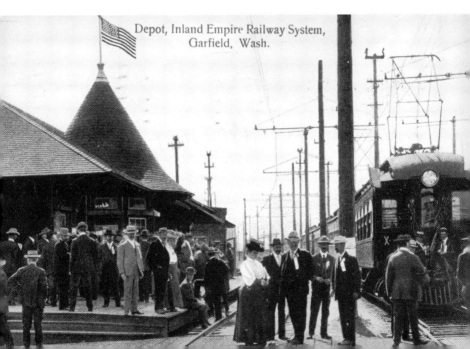

Interior of an S&IE parlor car, an alternative to the plush and wicker seats in coaches. Only longer trains and holiday runs included parlor cars. (*Electric Railroad Journal,* Oct. 8, 1910, 636)

The Coeur d'Alene division connected at Coeur d'Alene Lake with passenger and excursion vessels of the Red Collar line that plied the lake and the "shadowy" St. Joe River. (*Spokane's Electric Railroads,* S&IE)

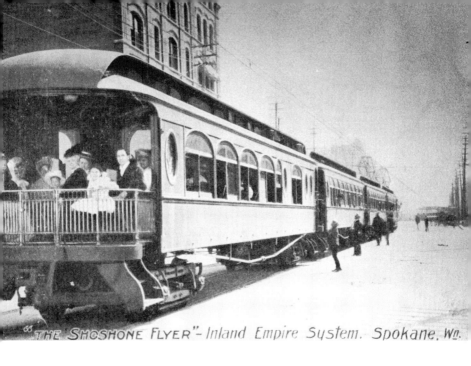

The "Shoshone Flyer," a crack S&IE passenger train on Main Avenue in Spokane, ready for its run. Graves employed a publicity man to place photos like this in newspapers and magazines. (*Spokane's Electric Railroads, S&IE*)

This view eastward on Main Avenue from the roof of the Spokane City Club shows the S&IE terminal building, which also served the Spokane Traction Company, at left. The tall buildings are the Auditorium (with tower), center, and Old National Bank (white) at right. (Author's collection)

Baseball game day at Recreation Park. Graves controlled the park, the streetcars, and for a time the professional team. (*Electric Railway Journal,* Feb. 27, 1909, 364)

One of the advertisements produced by S&IE publicity men to build up patronage to lake resorts developed by the railroad. The picture appeared in a trade journal article on railroad advertising techniques. (*Electric Railway Journal,* Oct. 8, 1910, 634)

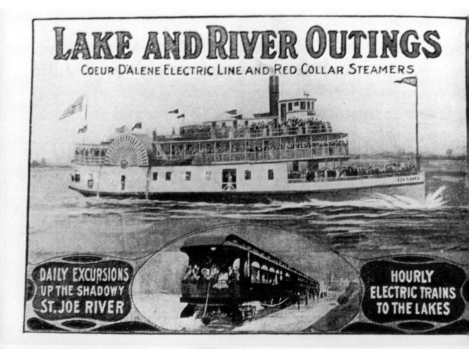

William H. Nichols, the New York copper refiner and chemist whose syndicate of noted copper men bought stock control of Granby Consolidated. (*World's Work,* 34 (Aug. 1917), 353)

Hillside cottages for managers at Anyox where Granby developed copper mines and smelter when the ores at Phoenix ran out. (Eugenia Howe collection, EWSHS)

Fred B. Grinnell, who had been a land buyer and right-of-way negotiator for the Great Northern, sold much of the Spokane city real estate that Graves developed. (Courtesy of John B. White, Jr., Sun City, Arizona)

Granby smelter at Anyox, overlooking Granby Bay, circa 1912. The company brought coal from Vancouver Island to fuel the smelter and dammed a creek for electrical current. (Author's collection)

Manito Park, the heart of Graves's development on Cook's Hill. Grand Boulevard, along which Graves planted five hundred trees, is at right, and the water tower, which the city built as a condition for developing the park, is in the distance. (Author's collection)

Manito Boulevard ran south from Manito Park with a parkway down the center. This view, at Twenty-Second and Manito Boulevard, shows the contoured streets laid out by Olmsted Brothers. (Allen Sperry collection, EWSHS)

Graves's mansion at Waikiki, near the Country Club, on the Little Spokane River. Designed by Kirtland K. Cutter, a fashionable Spokane architect, Waikiki was surrounded by model farms and a natural area for wild animals. (EWSHS No. L84-207.4.101)

Interior of Amanda Graves's sitting room at Waikiki. She assisted in its decoration and may have paid for the mansion with the sale of Spokane real estate. (Eugenia Howe collection, EWSHS)

Front entrance to Waikiki. Graves wanted an electrical gate installed so his chauffeur would not leave the auto to open it. He paid for the grading of a county road to his estate. (Roye photo, Eugenia Howe collection, EWSHS)

A recent view of Waikiki, which is operated as a meeting and retreat site by Gonzaga University. The extensive original grounds have been developed into residential sites. (Author's collection)

Graves in the academic robes he wore when Whitworth College awarded him an honorary Doctor of Laws degree. (Janice Howe family snapshot)

Jay Graves at his ease in the gardens at Waikiki. As long as the Graveses occupied Waikiki, they employed two or more gardeners. (Janice Howe family snapshot)

Left to right: Jay "Pierre" Graves, Alice, and Margaret Bean at the Graveses' home on Upper Terrace in Spokane. (Janice Howe family snapshot)

Four generations of Graveses: Jay Graves, right, holds his great-granddaughter, Janice; her father, Jay P. Graves II, center; and his father, Clyde Graves, right. (Janice Howe)

Whitworth College, 1938. Its first two buildings, Ballard and McMillan halls, are visible among the pines. (Whitworth College photo archives)

The Spokane & Inland Empire's first electric freight locomotive, with pantograph for country and trolley (tied down) for city travel. The name on the locomotive is that of the earlier company. (EWSHS No. 4070)

Holiday travelers at the Spokane terminal of the Spokane & Inland Empire. Both Traction Company trolley cars and the railroad's electric passenger trains ended their runs at the yellow building. (EWSHS No. 74-131)

The Spokane & Inland Empire used electric freight cars for mail and package deliveries along its lines. These were often coupled with passenger cars. (EWSHS No. 8690)

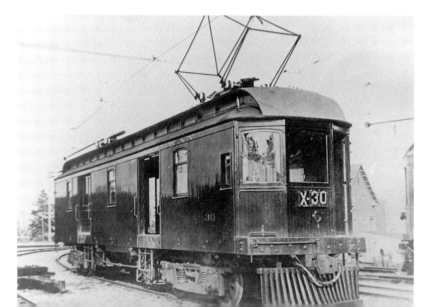

A construction locomotive on the Spokane & Inland Empire. The trestle crossed a portion of Moran Prairie, south of Spokane. Hiram Ferris is barely visible atop the locomotive, holding onto the bell. (EWSHS No. 5026)

Tracklaying on the Coeur d'Alene & Spokane, organized by F. A. Blackwell, which merged into the Spokane & Inland Empire as the Coeur d'Alene division. The scene is near the town of Coeur d'Alene. (EWSHS No. 3172)

Scene from a postcard inscribed: "Tragic wreck of the I.E. train near Coeur d'Alene during the Indian Land drawing rush of 1909." Photographer unknown. (EWSHS No. 3681)

Farm families waved from their fields as the Spokane & Inland Empire trains flashed past. Frequent, fast service enabled many rural passengers to visit Spokane and return in a day. (EWSHS No. 8689)

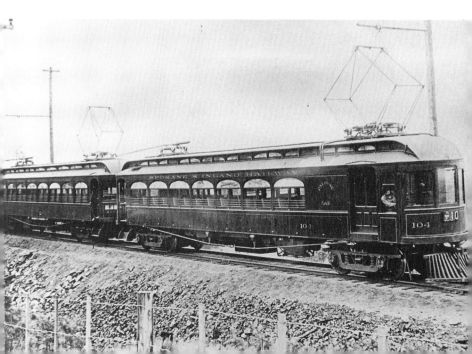

Prospective investors in Graves's railroad travel on benches nailed to a flatcar for a look at construction in the Palouse country. (EWSHS No. 8712)

Construction train of the Coeur d'Alene division being loaded with ballast gravel from a pit at Carnahan Road, east of Spokane. (EWSHS No. 8317)

earth—and marked by a cenotaph to the memory of Phoenix men who fell in battle.

Continual shortages of coke closed the Grand Forks smelter in 1919. It never ran again; its main buildings would be dismantled in 1921 to replace the surface structures of Hecla Mining Company, destroyed by fire at Burke, Idaho. Granby's vacant office and storage buildings, donated to the town of Grand Forks, would be used as a dump. With closure of the smelter, the company stopped paying dividends.

The company would extend its life and resume profitable operations, however, by means of the Copper Mountain mines on the Similkameen River, purchased in 1923 from Canada Copper Corporation, Ltd., and a mill at Allenby. Both shut down temporarily in the depression of the thirties. In 1971, faced with claims for unpaid national and provincial taxes, Granby sold stock control to Zapata Canada, a subsidiary of Zapata Corporation, a diversified tuna-fishing, marine, oil and gas exploration, and mining company based in Houston, Texas. Seven years later, Granby and Granisle, a subsidiary that mined copper open-pit in central British Columbia, amalgamated with Zapata.

James J. Hill died in May 1916. Graves resigned that year as a director and vice-president of Granby. He was fifty-seven years old. The company twice "had been on the brink of liquidation because of low prices and ore reserves," observed the *Western Miner,* but it eventually yielded the most copper of any in western Canada. "The story of Granby," the magazine said, "is a story of high risk, perseverance, frustration, luck, loyalty, intelligence and achievement." According to *Mining Age* of New York: the record of Granby "can hardly portray in adequate words the obstacles the company overcame." In Granby, Graves had beaten huge odds against success. Much of the perseverance, frustration, luck, and achievement had been his.[31]

CHAPTER 6

Changing Fortunes

Aubrey White's dream of a hilltop compound where he and Jay Graves would build chateaus on a promontory overlooking Southeast Boulevard animated him throughout 1909. He popped about Spokane whipping up support for a million-dollar park bond issue to carry out the Olmsted design; it would, with a new city charter, appear on the ballot in 1910.

As usual with Graves, the newspapers got wind of the chateau plan, calling the site "the most picturesque and striking landscape feature in Spokane," and Graves confirmed that he intended to build but laughed that his house would cost less than the $200,000 a reporter had heard. Building would wait, for the Jay and Clyde Graveses and the Whites were off to Pasadena for the winter.[1]

Clyde had married a Spokane bride, Blanche Flournoy, on January 26, 1906, and now there were two sons, Jay P. II, two years old, and the baby, Clyde Jr. White had married while he was in New York, and his wife, too, was a Spokane girl, Ethelyn, the daughter of John W. Binkley, a socially prominent and wealthy pioneer Spokane attorney who, with his partner, had managed the Hypotheekbank for Dutch investors until they had a falling out over fees. This was a jolly group bound for a winter holiday in the sunshine. The Graves men would spend much of their time at golf.

When the party returned to Spokane in the spring, however, White sensed that Graves's enthusiasm for the bluff site was cooling. When John C. Olmsted and Fred Dawson stopped in Spokane in April, Graves whisked them in his automobile to see his farm overlooking the Little Spokane River seven miles north of the city. He was talking about grading the county road, at his expense, from the city limits to his property and had started a company to produce macadam; he had permission from the county commissioners to re-route the road to suit his plans. As they walked along a bluff above the river, the three men discussed barns, paddock, bunkhouse for workmen, and so on. On their way back to town,

Olmsted told Graves that "if his place were near Boston, he could get a million dollars for it."[2]

Graves was turning the place into a model farm; he had 125 head of blooded Jersey cattle, purebred sheep, poultry, ninety acres of meadowland for hay, gardens on the hillsides, and a 100-horsepower electric plant on one of the springs. Olmsted thought the plant large enough to supply current for a big house and also to pump water into a reservoir to maintain lawns and gardens around it.

For some earthworks at the farm, Graves used crews and materials from the Spokane & Inland Empire. After Hill's people took the railroad, they billed Graves for $1,299 for this work; he demurred, arguing that "it tended toward the development of the Inland territory, and ... was done on the spare time of the engineers, when they would otherwise be doing nothing." By the time the railroad at last demanded payment, the statute of limitations had overtaken the alleged debt.[3]

Flush from selling the Spokane & Inland Empire system to Hill, Graves had decided to build a home at his farm, which he named Waikiki ("many waters") for a favored Hawaiian resort. He engaged the Olmsted firm to landscape extensive grounds, and the local architect, Kirtland Cutter, to design a dignified manor on a bluff overlooking the Little Spokane.

Graves also had enough money to lend $125,000 to Spokane's most exclusive men's fraternity, the Spokane Club, which gave him, as collateral, a mortgage on its new home, also designed by Cutter's firm, a four-story Georgian red brick clubhouse about to be erected on the northwest corner of Riverside and Monroe. (The club's library, paneled in mahogany, would have a walk-in fireplace second in size only to the one in Seattle's Rainier Club, also designed by Cutter.)[4]

The Spokane Club building cost so much that the club issued bonds secured by a second mortgage, junior to Graves's, to the Spokane and Eastern Trust Company. The Elks Spokane lodge bought bonds of this second mortgage, and when the Spokane Club could not make timely payment on its notes to Graves, the Elks contracted with Graves to buy the building. Only by reorganizing as the Spokane City Club and buying its own structure at a sheriff's sale was the club able to keep its quarters.[5]

For a time, Graves wanted a house for Clyde beside his at Waikiki with a four-car garage between them. Letters coursed back and forth between Olmsted in Brookline, Cutter in Spokane, and Graves wherever he happened to be, changing this pathway and that garden. The Olmsted firm resorted to finding Graves through C. A. Smith, his secretary. From The Maryland in Pasadena, Graves sent a note to Dawson that he had acquired the "Dart farm" east of his barns for a road Dawson had recommended; on his typewritten note, Graves for no apparent reason penned a tart comment: "Hotel stenographers are not experts."[6]

Aubrey White, in the meantime, was in full cry after parklands. His method for acquiring them was to assemble a group of his wealthy supporters, show them the ground he wanted, and ask them to buy and donate it to the park system. He called these men his "powerhouse"—such men as the newspaper publisher, William H. Cowles; the restaurant proprietor who was soon to front for a syndicate that would build a hotel, Louis M. Davenport; the securities broker Joel E. Ferris (Frank Graves's brother-in-law); Robert Lewis Rutter, president of the Spokane and Eastern Trust Company; and John Finch, mineowner and real estate speculator. Often Cowles would treat the powerhouse to lunch and then drive them to see White's proposed parkland.

A million-dollar bond issue, passed by a margin of eighteen ballots (although a court challenge reduced the available monies to $875,000), permitted White and the park board to also buy desirable land for parks, scenic drives, and vistas. By 1913, largely following a plan Dawson wrote in the name of Olmsted Brothers, the park board had acquired 1,480.59 acres, most of the land White had earmarked for park use.[7]

As Graves prepared to move into his estate at Waikiki, White bought his nine-year-old Georgian revival mansion at First and Hemlock in Browne's Addition. There he could settle his family and garden in the large grounds. Graves sold for $50,000, taking White's four-year-old ten-room house at Ninth and Monroe as $15,000 of the price. But White's finances were showing a strain; a letter he wrote from Santa Barbara to Dawson, who had made a plan for White's garden, was testy: "I confess that I find all of your profession seem to think clients can dig the necessary cash somewhere on their grounds, and do not try to make the plans or the costs as economical as they might." He went on about future taxes on his property. And before he moved into the Graves house, White had offered it back to Graves as security for a $20,000 loan.⁸

For Graves's farm, Cutter designed a two-and-one-half-story English revival mansion with a main wing ninety feet long surmounting the bluff above the river, a service wing at an angle on the east, and a loggia on the west opening onto a formal sunken garden. The exterior walls of cream stucco were half-timbered; the long roof line was varied by gables and four chimneys, three false and one functional, the real one rising from a double fireplace that opened on a library on one side and a living room on the other. Cutter drew Tudor arched doorways and varisized paneled windows, casement and sash, and large plate windows on the north to overlook the river and a lower terrace.⁹

Graves demanded a model of house and grounds which was sent to him in California. With this, and data from Olmsted and Cutter, he began suggesting changes; when bids came for various parts of the work, he scaled some down and questioned others. The projected cost of a formal garden, $10,000, was twice his estimate; he asked for a new plan. He mulled for weeks over a rock entrance to the estate, one with "an electrical contrivance" that would allow his chauffeur to open and close the gate without getting out of the auto. Cutter and Dawson patiently answered his questions and produced new drawings, and the new house began to take shape. It was to be occupied by Christmas 1912. Cutter labeled his elevations "country home of Mr. J. P. Graves," but in fact it would be Graves's only home for a decade, and well before he moved in, he adopted a letterhead: Waikiki Farm, on the Little Spokane, J. P. Graves, owner.¹⁰

The plan for Clyde's adjoining house was soon dropped, although Graves kept the four-car garage, with a small outbuilding for his office between garage and house. He had mentioned a total of $100,000 to Dawson, but the special bricks, millwork, electrical system, and decoration ran past that figure: the general contract was more than $85,000, the millwork, $9,000, interior decorating, $14,000, and so on. Since Graves had his own generating plant, the electrical contractor was instructed to install numerous outlets for vacuum cleaners, electric irons, a washing machine, and other appliances (in a day when Graves's few neighbors burned kerosene lamps), and four private telephone stations.¹¹

Above the loggia, Cutter sketched the mandatory billiard room.

(Unlike many of the architect's Spokane clients, Graves did not order a ballroom.) How much Amanda Graves contributed to the general plan is uncertain. (Possibly the proceeds of her sale of a commercial site to Shaw and Borden, a printing and office supply house, for $210,000 paid for the house.) Certainly she approved Cutter's plans, and in her private quarters she called for flowered wall fabric, full-length mirrored closets along one entire wall, and tiered hat racks in a closet on another wall. The master bath contained a marble shower with ranks of ringed spray valves that thoroughly doused the bather. The Graveses ordered elegant furniture and specially designed silverware.

As building progressed, however, the Olmsted firm discovered uneasily that, while Graves was quick to make changes, he was slow to pay. Dawson, in frustration, wrote from San Diego to the home office: "Better send a letter to Graves and say that we would be glad to know why he hasn't paid our bill in full and have *FLO sign it*. He has no right to juggle things just has [sic] he thinks and make a plaything out of us. . . . I don't want to put the fees any lower as he is mighty unsatisfactory to do business with because he is too impatient and because we are so far away we cannot give him proper attention." Dawson suggested that, if Graves did not pay, the Olmsteds should "write him tendering our resignation."[12]

Some years later, John Olmsted inquired about the value of Spokane & Inland Empire stock he had taken in payment for some of the work. Graves's bland reply, in part: "I am sorry to say that we were large losers in this company as well as others, but that seems to have been the history of electric railway corporations."[13]

Graves's money was going largely into land at this time; he was buying ground in parcels of forty acres or more east and southeast of Waikiki with the notion of developing new suburban residential lots or irrigated tracts. White and Clyde Graves also acquired land in the area, most of it contiguous with Jay Graves's. By the end of 1912, he held perhaps 3,000 acres north of Spokane, largely open country that had been logged by lumber companies or passed over by home seekers who saw better farmland elsewhere. Here and there Graves's land speckled with attractive treed sections, hills that blazed with spring and summer flowers, and arresting vistas. Touched by the skill of an Olmsted, this ground might blossom.

Consequently, on July 15, 1912, Graves organized the Country Homes Development Company with White and Clyde. (He had first thought to call it the "Suburban" company but, in the articles of incorporation, lined out the word and penned "Country Homes" instead, evoking images of space and quietude.) The company's purposes were to plat and develop real estate, build electrical and water-pumping plants and distribution systems, and, of course, buy, sell, and hold land. When the company chose its officers, the three stockholders naturally elected Jay Graves president and White and Clyde first vice-presidents; C. A. Shuff became secretary, and Graves's secretary, C. A. Smith, treasurer. Shuff, an attorney who had been with Graves in the Spokane-Washington Improvement and Hayden Lake companies, also emerged as untitled manager of the company.[14]

Marketing irrigated tracts impressed Graves as unpromising. Irrigation promotions had sprung up along every likely creek in eastern Washington; more than half a dozen irrigation districts speckled the Spokane Valley, east of the city; and not far north of Graves's land, Arcadia, a company organized only a few years earlier to establish irrigated orchards, foundered in debt.

Graves no longer could command a railway line to his land, but he proposed to pave roads and establish auto-bus service. He needed an incentive for buyers, a lure to lift his ground above competing sites, and he found it—or more properly it found him—in the survival struggles of Whitworth College, a Presbyterian school in Tacoma.

The Spokane Presbytery, invited to join other sects in opening a Christian college in Spokane, charged a committee with investigating the proposal, and the committee instead recommended continued support of Whitworth. But it also went to Country Homes Development to suggest that, if land were donated, Whitworth might move to Spokane. The Presbyterians' "overtures were met sympathetically," and after several conferences with Graves and his sales manager, the committee framed a proposal (which Graves patently helped write) to Country Homes: "This committee desires to bring to your attention the desirability of locating this institution" on Graves's land, where "musicals, lectures, and other college interests together with a clean social atmosphere would attract many desirable citizens to locate here." (One of the most vocal members of the committee, incidentally, was "Professor" John F. Saylor, proprietor of a school for boys, who doubtless saw opportunity for himself in a nearby college.)[15]

Whitworth had been founded by George F. Whitworth, who had gone to Olympia in 1854 to settle a Presbyterian colony and open a school. He moved on to Sumner, where he started an academy in 1884; in 1890, he enlarged the academy, made it a college, and gave it his name. The panic of 1893 nearly sank Whitworth's school; he received offers to move it, and in 1899 he relocated it to the Tacoma estate of the late Allan C. Mason, who had failed in the depression trying to carry his debtors through the hard times. Closed for a time by lack of students, Whitworth College, with fewer than 200 enrolled, was hanging on gamely in 1913; its total assets, excluding equipment, amounted to about $151,000, and its endowment, targeted for $250,000, seemed stalled at $108,000. Tacoma's citizens had tired of appeals for support, and the college's trustees had been looking for a "more strategic location with a larger territory [which] would . . . more likely commend it to Eastern givers."[16]

Graves offered the college board and the Synod of Washington, under whose jurisdiction it fell, a strategy: he would set aside one entire section, 640 acres, for the college, 40 to be used as campus, 40 more directly east to be marketed as residential sites "as rapidly as possible for a building fund," and the balance, 560, to be platted as homesites from which Whitworth would receive 45 percent of sales revenue if Graves's company sold the lots or 55 percent if the college or its friends sold them. After ten years, Whitworth could buy any unsold lots for a price to be negotiated. Graves, who claimed to have invested $700,000 in land and improvements for Country Homes, suggested that Whitworth's land—campus and homesites—was worth approximately $350,000.[17]

To move, however, the college board would need funds to build classrooms and dormitories; it therefore asked that Spokane citizens contribute $100,000 as a condition for relocating. A number of the city's prominent businessmen—Edwin Coman and Fielding McClaine, bankers; Robert Paterson of the Crescent department store; Cowles; David Brown, John Porter, Thomas Humbird and August Paulsen among them—joined Presbyterian ministers, elders, and of course Graves and Saylor in a campaign to raise the funds.

Calvin H. French, secretary of the national Presbyterian College Board, came out from New York to direct the drive, and by the end of April 1913, with approximately $80,000 pledged, a Spokane delegation of businessmen and college trustees went to Tacoma to "insist" that Spokane's offer be accepted. On September 26, 1913, the college's board recommended moving to Spokane, and on October 16, the Synod concurred. (Although the drive had fallen short, the Synod voted to contribute $30,000.) In the meantime, Graves had increased the land designated for a campus to 100 acres.[18]

A small group of supporters gathered on May 22, 1914, at groundbreaking for a $30,000 building; by mid-summer, a second had been started. Whitworth College opened on its Spokane campus on September 23 with forty students.

Graves's Country Homes Development Company transferred the promised land to Whitworth on December 10, 1914, with a stipulation in the deed (requested by the Presbytery) that no intoxicating liquors be vended and no commercial buildings erected on the campus. The Presbytery voted a resolution: We "commend to all our people the purchase of suitable lots, the proceeds of which are to be largely used in the building up of our Synodical College."[19]

Jay Graves, describing himself as "retired," was named one of the twenty-four trustees; he would remain on the board for the rest of his life, chairing it for a time and serving in campaigns to raise money. He also headed the buildings and grounds committee and, in that capacity, ambled across campus to select this space for lawn and that for shrubbery, planted an avenue of Hawthorne trees, and set out locusts. Although the college closed temporarily during World War I, its buildings housed an army auto-tractor school.

Graves gave the college a house and lot in Spokane, valued at $6,500, to sell. Gradually Whitworth revived after the war; its enrollment would exceed 200 by 1938, and it would mount a building program in 1940 with the appointment of Dr. Frank F. Warren as president. Warren struggled against the shortages of another war, buying nails by the pound from country hardware stores to complete a gymnasium named Graves Hall.[20]

Once assured of a college on his ground, Graves put on the market the first group of homesites, Spokane Estates, directly south of the campus, between the city and the college, platting generous lots 100 feet or more wide and roughly 300 feet deep along curved or angled streets. The Spokane Country Club was laying out an eighteen-hole course immediately west of Graves's farm, on down Waikiki Road from Graves's stone-pillared entrance. Graves and D. W. Twohy were vice-presidents of the club and, once the links opened, Graves would play there often; he had grown fond of golf.

A caddy for Graves remembers him as polite and even-tempered but not a generous tipper. The going caddy rate for a round was $1.20. Jay often played with his brother Frank, who puffed cigars continually; and on number 10, with a steep climb to the green, Frank held onto one end of a club, short of breath, while his caddy took the other to pull him uphill.[21]

Nearby, Waikiki continued to develop as a model farm. Graves bought and raised purebred livestock and poultry, cultivated crops, and operated a dairy to provide breeding stock. He exhibited his prize Jerseys often at livestock shows and fairs. His 700-acre farm also embraced a game park: a wild area for deer and an artificial lake for wildfowl. His men clipped the wings of swans and wood ducks so they could not fly away. Graves imported swans from Massachusetts for breeding, a pair of Reeves pheasants for $85, a pair of Amherst pheasants for $100, and more. Waikiki was, Graves pointed out, "not owned and kept up for purposes of profit but as a model farm . . . for the pleasure of its owner . . . and everyone is at liberty to ride, drive or walk through the place." He was outraged when a zealous game warden arrested him for killing deer from his herd and accused the warden of depriving him of his property without due process. His complaint reached the state supreme court, where the justices ruled that the animals and birds, in which Graves had invested $5,000, were indeed his but he might not "dispose of them in such a manner as he sees fit."[22]

Graves would use his demonstration farm, he announced, to teach proper dairying methods to settlers on his development, Milan Farms, logged-off land priced at $8 to $20 an acre and irrigated from lakes, near the hamlet of Milan (pronounced "my land") about two and one-half miles north of Waikiki. With officers of the lumber firm that logged the land, Washington Mill Company, Graves and White organized the Milan Farms Development Company in August 1913, naming Clyde Graves as general manager. Here, said Jay Graves, he would encourage settlers to raise hogs, livestock, and dairy cows by offering them thoroughbred breeding animals from his own herds. His enthusiasm for this scheme was only temporarily dampened by the necessity of destroying nearly half his milk cows after rabid dogs bit them. Graves stormed to city hall to demand that "every dog in this city should be muzzled, confined or destroyed," and for a time, the city (although Graves's farm was outside its limits) required dogs to be muzzled.[23]

With a college, a country club, a model farm, and the promise of breeding stock as attractions, Graves seemed well set to sell his ground north of Spokane. But sales lagged. Graves pledged some of the platted land to the Union Trust Company for loans to keep his real estate enterprise afloat. Occasionally he bought a little more acreage next to some he already owned. But between 1913 and 1919, the Country Homes Development Company sold only fifteen homesites, and Milan Farms, about half a dozen.

The market for residential property had gone flat. Residential tracts, despite full-page advertisements in the newspapers and promotions touting last-chance bargains, lay empty all over Spokane and environs. In its great surge of construction to house the hordes flooding the city up to 1910, Spokane had overbuilt.

One casualty of the slowdown in housing was Graves's old compatriot, Aubrey White. "I regret that the continued dull financial conditions in this section of the country makes it impossible for me to liquidate the principal of this note," he wrote Olmsted Brothers in 1915, "but you may rest assured that I will do so at my first opportunity." Graves, too, was pinched: in 1912 he took White's renewed note for $20,000 on the house he had sold him in Spokane, and, when White could not pay on time, apparently forced a sale. This would be remembered by both families as a falling out.[24]

White moved out of town to his father-in-law's farm, Montvale, on the Little Spokane. Leaving the city cost him his place on the park board, but he wrote Fred Dawson cheerfully that he was now "a real farmer." White would make Montvale a showplace and try to earn a living at other work. His attempts to sell paint and wallpaper and to broker stocks failed, however, and his friend Cowles eventually made a place for him as garden editor of the *Spokesman-Review,* where he carried on his campaign for civic beautification, chafing that, because he did not type, his copy passed through a public stenographer.

Graves auctioned unsold lots in a "mammoth tent" on October 1, 1921, luring prospective bidders out with automobiles from town. About thirty-five sales resulted, and shortly after, Graves replatted the tract as Country Homes Estates with 229 available lots. These would be sold for $250 to $400—"a delightful home site located within 20 minutes ride from the center of Spokane . . . well kept paved highways"—as one-, two-, and five-acre sites.[25]

With his money largely tied up in real estate, Graves's finances tottered; he wrote one mortgage to pay another. Clyde and his wife spent enough time on the links to become championship golfers, but Blanche died in the flu epidemic of 1918, and Clyde married a woman the family considered "an adventuress." It was a brief union; he would marry a third time.

Amanda Graves had been suffering for four years from a heart ailment that restricted her social life, confining her to Waikiki until her heart failed altogether on the last day of November 1920. She had not been dead many months when Jay Graves remarried: Mary Alice Hardin Towne, a widow twenty years younger than he, whom he had met some years earlier at The Maryland in Pasadena. She came as the second Mrs. Graves to Waikiki, a demanding presence in the mansion that Amanda had enjoyed so briefly.[26]

Graves's family—son and grandchildren—liked Alice. They called her Dearest in conversation and letters. And when she learned that Jay used no middle name, she called him Pierre, her affectionate name for her husband. Always solicitous of family, Graves made sure that she got her household allowance even when he had to ask the staff to wait for their pay. (New employees were cautioned, "Don't talk back to Mr. Graves." Or to Alice, either.) Staff members—usually two maids, a cook, two gardeners, and a chauffeur—suspected that Alice did not know Graves's real financial situation, although more probably they misread her stratagems for sparing his feelings. Like Graves, Dearest was a native of Illinois, from Fulton, about 100 miles north of Carthage; she was hardy, lively, and out going; she circulated in Spokane society; she was president of the landscape association of St. John's Cathedral (Episcopal), an appointment of social standing. When the Graveses dined with the Davenports, also a social indicator, Jay Graves wrote in the guest register, "Swell groceries."[27]

While his real estate sales lagged, Graves cast about for a mine that might restore his fortune. Even though western lead and silver mining was depressed by rising costs and a market largely controlled by one smelting combine, a promising claim always stirred speculators. White, Graves, and Walter Nicholls, a broker, formed a company to take over the old Cleveland mine in northeast Washington. The Cleveland's silver-lead ore, carrying antimony, iron, and bismuth, had always been difficult to process, and Graves ran out of capital for it in 1918. White and Nicholls, with William

Yolen Williams, had also taken the Eden-Crescent near Ainsworth, British Columbia, but it came to nothing.

Graves's old alchemy betrayed him; he could not easily raise capital after investors' losses in the Spokane & Inland Empire bonds, and he had forfeited others' confidence in trying to sell the Spokane Club building to the Elks. Now, with thin capital, the fate of each mine was the same: it would open with high hopes, time would pass, some funds dribbled for improvements, and the ore or money would run out. Thus, Midas in Montana, Columbia Mines Corporation and Spokane-Idaho Copper Company with thirty claims in the Hoodoo district, Moscow Queen near Moscow, Ten-Said near Potlatch—all in Latah County, Idaho—failed; and there were others.

In the business doldrums following the war, Walter Nicholls, who had been brokering Graves's forays into mining, went bankrupt, costing Graves $23,089 he could not afford to lose. Graves, with other clients, sued, but there was no money to be recovered. "A bucketshop," he raged.[28]

Graves's most promising mining ventures were the Seven Troughs Reorganized Mining Company, which attempted to revive an old gold-silver mine near Lovelock, Nevada, and the Constitution, a limping silver mine consistently hampered by lack of capital, in the Pine Creek district west and south of Wardner, scene of early lead-silver discoveries in northern Idaho.

In grazing country marked with cattle-watering troughs that gave the company its name, Seven Troughs yielded ore for its original operators from 1906 to 1917, when underground water flows forced closure. It had been idle almost a decade when Graves sampled the ore, made the mandatory optimistic pronouncements, and set about unwatering the old mine. But workers hit only pockets of mineral, never a vein, and his hopes for new capital were dashed by the stock market crash of 1929.[29]

The Constitution, operated before Graves's entry by a company headed by George Turner and Frank T. Post, veteran Spokane attorneys, was conceded to hold commercial lead and zinc ores but had never been adequately financed. Graves, having lost his connections with eastern backers, resorted to asking Robert Rutter, the banker, to write him a letter of introduction to the manager of the credit department of the Chase Bank in Paris.

"Few of our citizens have ever done big things in a big way, on a scale equal to his," Rutter wrote. "Wide experience in both the financing, and the operation of mining properties, coupled with unusual contacts among business men of the foremost type, give him a background to carry on the development of the Constitution with unusual hope for success." No money came from Paris. Graves installed a new plant, but the depression of the thirties sank the Constitution.[30]

With each venture, the newspapers recalled what Graves had been: promoter of Granby, builder of railroads, and so on, flattering each new plunge. In fact, Graves's resources trickled away in the twenties; he sold livestock to pay for trips and for sojourns in Pasadena (the Graveses now favored a playground of the rich and famous, the Huntington Hotel), and he pledged his land for loans. The sticky loans were two, one for $12,500 and the other for $30,000, from Prudential Insurance, both incurred in 1923 with his home and farm as security.[31]

He and Alice rented a house in Hawaii near the Oahu Country Club in 1926. He golfed nearly every day. While the Graveses were gone, officers of the Union Trust Company, an old National Bank subsidiary—Twohy, George L. Kimmel, and attorneys—went through Waikiki to appraise his assets for sale; the trust company did not seize Waikiki but put Kimmel in charge of Country Homes Estates and Milan Farms, taking them out of Graves's hands.[32]

The years 1926–34 were lean by Graves's standards. He had to let much of the farm help go, pay some employees with mining stock, and drive his own auto (a 1924 Nash) except on long trips; and he was struggling to bring his Hoodoo mines into production.

By 1934, Graves clearly could not maintain Waikiki; the family of three—Alice's widowed aunt, Mary A. Justice, had come to live with them—moved to number 210 in the Roosevelt Apartments in Spokane. Alice gamely told her friends that Waikiki had been too confining, too "isolated" from the social life she enjoyed, but the Graveses packed picnic baskets for reminiscent visits to the mansion and grounds on sunny afternoons.

Margaret Bean, daughter of a pioneer family and now a featured writer and critic for the *Spokesman-Review,* frequently joined them for outings; she was fond of them and they of her; she admired Graves (he was 75 and she, like a daughter, 44) and, knowing what he had achieved, was saddened to see that they "sold most of their furniture [for money] to live on." She wrote several appreciative articles about his career for the newspaper, some based on her conversations with him, enlarging the legend of his past triumphs.

To settle his debts, Graves at last reluctantly sold Waikiki and its remaining grounds in 1937 for $53,500 to Charles E. Marr of Spokane, wealthy from the merger of grocery chains. Graves was thus able to pay off the Prudential mortgages and to build another home in Spokane, a two-story cream stucco of twelve rooms on Upper Terrace, overlooking Rockwood Boulevard. The house was designed by the architectural firm Rigg and Vantyne. Archibald Rigg had been one of the few owners, twenty years before, of a homesite in Country Homes (perhaps taken in payment for architectural work). The Graveses' new neighbors did not welcome them; they complained that he destroyed stately trees, planted during his development of this section three decades earlier, and erected an "ugly" retaining wall.[33]

Graves approached eighty. He had not scored a significant business success in thirty years. Clyde, the son he had hoped would carry on, had been working for the Federal Housing Administration; he died in 1941. Graves moved in a constricting circle of Whitworth College and family, spending winters in Pasadena unless illness kept him home. To his great-granddaughter, Janice, whose father was Jay II, he was a frail, kindly man with a wonderful chiming pocket watch she climbed onto his lap to hear.

On June 29, 1946, Dearest wrote Janice a short letter: "Your great grandfather Graves and I are dismantling our home to live in our hotel in southern California. . . . You are too young, as a little girl, to receive this chest of silver. It is our wish that you receive it, as our gift, on your happy wedding day." It was, of course, the Gorham pattern struck especially for Waikiki by the New York firm of Marcus and Company thirty-five years earlier, a remembrance of Graves's glory days.[34]

Jay P. Graves died peacefully, aged eighty-eight, in the Huntington Hotel on the morning of April 27, 1948. His older brother, Frank, whom he had followed to Spokane, had died four months earlier. To his wife, Jay left an estate consisting of $110 worth of personal items, the valueless stock of six mining companies, and 60,000 shares in the Spokane-Idaho Mining Company, which she sold before probate, with the court's approval, for $45,000 to invest largely in United States certificates. The couple also had a joint bank account with a balance of $10,867.76. He had known he was dying on February 8 last when he signed, with a shaky hand, his final testament, two short paragraphs.[35]

As Jay Graves wished, his ashes were scattered on the Whitworth campus. Dearest had been too ill to attend the little memorial service in President Warren's study "where two perfectly gorgeous boquets [sic] of red roses filled the room with color." "After prayer," Warren wrote her, "we went over to the east side of the campus overlooking the beautiful valley below which once belonged to Mr. Graves, and there . . . Jay P. Graves II [Clyde's elder son] distributed the ashes." Margaret Bean had been there, too, and she wrote Alice, "I did everything I could to give the dear Skipper all the recognition the paper could give him."[36]

And she added, "Do you remember a place behind the college where we picked flowers one Sunday? You and the Skipper and I? It overlooked Mt. Spokane and the lower part of Waikiki . . . remote, peaceful, and full of wild flowers. That is where we put the ashes. . . . They fell on a bed of little star flowers. . . . And I had a feeling that the Skipper would have been most happy to have his last earthly memory in that beautiful spot."

Notes

In the following notes, I use about three dozen abbreviations for recurring persons, publications, and agencies. I also make parentheses do double duty, in some cases to identify the location of a source cited, and in others to link a portion of the narrative to its source.

The abbreviations and their meanings are, in alphabetical order:

AR	Annual report, with year
ARET	Adams Real Estate Trust
BCM	British Columbia Minister of Mines annual report, with year
CFA2	Charles Francis Adams II
Chr	*Spokane Chronicle* or *Daily Chronicle*
CPR	Canadian Pacific Railroad
Dir(s)	Spokane City Directory (or Directories), with year
Durham	Nelson W. Durham, *History of the City of Spokane and Spokane Country* . . . with volume
EMJ	*Engineering and Mining Journal*
ERJ	*Electric Railway Journal*
EWSHS	Eastern Washington State Historical Society
EWU	Eastern Washington University
GAIA	Glenbow-Alberta Institute Archives
GFG	*Grand Forks* (B.C.) *Gazette* or *News-Gazette*
GN	Great Northern Railway
GN Pres	Great Northern President's files, Minnesota Historical Society
Hill	James Jerome Hill Reference Library
JCO	John C. Olmsted
K-L	Kiernan-Lawyer
LC	Library of Congress
Mass HS	Massachusetts Historical Society
Minn HS	Minnesota Historical Society
NA	National Archives of the United States
NP	Northern Pacific Railroad or Railway

NP Pres Northern Pacific President's files, Minnesota Historical Society
NYT   *New York Times*
PABC   Provincial Archives of British Columbia
PAC   Public Archives of Canada
Poor's   RR or Industrials, Poor's annual manuals, with year
S#O   Thomas G. Shaughnessy letterbook, with number
S&IE   Spokane & Inland Empire Railroad
SR   *Spokesman-Review* (Spokane)
WSU   Washington State University
WWP   Washington Water Power Company

Deeds and mortgages from Spokane County records are identified by book and page—e.g., 23:333 means book 23, page 333—and in some cases by a file number assigned by the county. The file number generally indicates that I read the deed in the file of a property owner rather than in county registers.

CHAPTER 1: BOUNDARY

1. Adam Smith, *Wealth of Nations,* 423.
2. *SR* Sept. 14, 1913.
3. *SR* June 3, 1901. The principal Montreal investor was R. R. Macaulay. He and Graves also put money into the Rockland group in Slocan camp. For further details of the LeRoi, see the author's *Inland Empire: D. C. Corbin and Spokane,* 171–72. Church, "Mining Companies" (pp. 309, 376, 401), shows Pope in the California Gold Mining Co., head office, Spokane, and Graves, secretary-treasurer, indicating that the Big Three office was also Spokane. Pope also appears to have invested in the original Old Ironsides, 156, but does not appear in Graves's later mining companies.
4. *Dir* 1896 shows Palmerston, a miner, living in the Review Hotel. Some accounts say four men discovered Old Ironsides and Knob Hill. Packhorse: *SR* Sept. 14, 1913.
5. White in *SR* Jan. 15, 1928; April 4, 1896; Edward J. Roberts recalled the poker game. According to deed indexes, Graves was inactive in real estate in 1896 but was president 1895–99 of the Washington Abstract and Title Guarantee Co., Spokane. The start of development is based on a historical review in Granby AR 1910, p. 10.
6. *SR* Jan. 1, 1896; *Mining Record,* 7:9 (Sept. 1900), 335–39, describes

B.C. Copper Co., and Church shows it registered in British Columbia on April 26, 1898, with offices in New York and Anaconda, B.C.

7. The phrase "surface showings" is interesting in this context because Boundary deposits lay generally under several feet of topsoil. *SR* Oct. 27, 1896.

8. White in *SR* Jan. 15, 1928.

9. *Montreal Herald,* June 9, 10, 1911 (quotation, June 9); *Montreal Gazette,* June 10, 1911; Morgan, *Canadian Men and Women of the Time,* 810.

10. Miner's resources, *Canada 1893,* 396, a handbook of business. The Eastern Townships Bank was a strong institution established in 1859.

11. No copy of Linsley's report was located, but it was generously quoted in *GFG* Aug. 11, 1906. See O. E. LeRoy, *Memoir 21,* and C. M. Campbell, Canadian Mining Institute *Transactions* 22 (1919), 155–79, geology of area.

12. On Whitaker Wright, see author's *Inland Empire: D. C. Corbin and Spokane,* 183–86; J. A. Eagle, *Canadian Pacific Railroad and . . . Western Canada,* 235, discusses the relationship between the War Eagle buyers and the Canadian Pacific based on letters of the principals.

13. Graves to Shaughnessy, May 18, 1899 (CPR), mentioning earlier contacts. The *Spokesman-Review,* Oct. 20, 1897, published a dispatch quoting the CPR president, Sir William Van Horne, as proposing a line from Robson to Fraser by way of Boundary.

14. Order in Council, Aug. 8, 1898, authorizing lease of Columbia & Western (PAC RG43, subj. 726). Columbia & Western, built by F. A. Heinze, had a land grant. Both Shaughnessy and Graves negotiated to purchase railroad lands from Heinze: Shaughnessy to J. S. Dennis, B.C. land commissioner, April 10, 1903 (S#80). Among a number of accounts of British Columbia's quest for rails are: Barman, *West beyond the West,* 176–82, 199–200, and Turner, *Sternwheelers and Steam Tugs, passim.* Eagle, *Canadian Pacific Railroad and . . . Western Canada,* 120–21, discusses the Columbia & Western in the hands of the Canadian Pacific. When Premier James Dunsmuir came to office in 1900, he signed a preliminary pact with the railroad contractors William McKenzie and Donald Mann to build the Vancouver, Victoria & Eastern. They had built part of the Canadian Northern, and Mann was among contractors who laid CPR from Robson to Midway. Shaughnessy believed the VV&E was intended for sale to Hill from its inception.

15. The Crow's Nest Pass agreement of June 29, 1897, allowed the CPR $11,000 a mile from Dominion and 20,000 acres a mile from the

provincial government; it also ceded coal lands to the railroad and gave concessions on rates. See Eagle, *Canadian Pacific Railroad and . . . Western Canada,* 44–49, on the Crow's Nest Pass agreement. It satisfied no one.

16. *Telephone Talk,* Aug. 1918, a photocopy in Cominco file, PABC; *SR* Nov. 30, 1899.

17. Under an agreement closed by J. P. Morgan, the Great Northern acquired the SF&N from the Northern Pacific on July 1, 1898; see *133 ICC Reports* 308–13.

18. The Soo is the Minneapolis, St. Paul & Sault Ste. Marie road. See Hidy and Hidy, *Great Northern,* 97–98. Letters related to Hill's plans include: Hill to D. S. Lamont, July 17, 1898, to Ledoux July 28, 1898, and Morgan & Co. to Hill, Oct. 8, 1898, and W. Thompson to Hill, March 8, 1899 (Hill).

19. CPR president in *Vancouver News Advertiser,* Oct. 29, 1899, quoted by Sanford, *McCulloch's Wonder,* 245 n.22.

20. O. B. Smith, Jr., to Graves, July 15, 1910; historical summary in Granby AR 1910; BCM 1899, p. 768.

21. In the organization, Miner emerged as the largest shareholder with 666,667, Gault with 604,066, and Graves with 450,000. They were directors of Granby, along with James H. McKechnie, a partner with Miner in a Granby (Quebec) gristmill, Fayette Brown, Montreal insurance agent, Aubrey White, and William Yolen Williams.

22. *SR* Feb. 25, 1910, May 13, 1949; C. Hanbury-Williams, *Blackwood's,* April 1903, p. 507 (quotation); *Phoenix Pioneer,* special edition, January 1904.

23. *Phoenix Pioneer,* January 1904.

24. PABC microfilm reel 4417; White in *SR* Jan. 15, 1928.

25. Hodges's biography, *GFG* March 3, 1910; Aldridge to Shaughnessy, Dec. 28, 1898 (CPR).

26. EMJ 70:22 (Dec. 1, 1900), 636.

27. Graves to Shaughnessy, June 22, 1899; Tye to Shaughnessy, June 24, 1899 (CPR).

28. Aldridge to Shaughnessy, Aug. 3, 1899 (CPR), attaching a proposed rate schedule with supporting data from his survey of U.S. railroads and smelters.

29. *SR* Nov. 27, 1899; *Mining Record,* 7 (1900), 207 ff., has a detailed description of the smelting works with diagrams and photographs.

30. The smelter spur cost $56,000: W. W. Colpitts to Shaughnessy, Aug. 5, 1899, and Aldridge to Shaughnessy, Oct. 7, 1899; Graves to

Shaughnessy, May 15, 1899, and to Tye, June 12, 1899 (all CPR); *SR* Dec. 18, 1899.

31. *Phoenix Pioneer,* April 14, 1900. Schwantes, *Radical Heritage,* 123, identifies the Phoenix unit as a radical union. Granby's compliance: *Phoenix Pioneer,* Feb. 24 and 27, 1900; Granby AR 1910, 11.

32. Ramsey, *Ghost Towns of B.C.,* 177–78, quoting Boundary County Historical Society AR.

33. *Wave,* 1899, published in San Francisco (PABC); *SR* Nov. 30, 1899; EMJ 71:9 (March 2, 1901), 286.

34. Eastern Townships Bank AR 1901, 384; *Phoenix Pioneer,* June 16, 1900; Rudin, *Banking en français,* 91–94. The branching to Boundary began the transformation of the bank from a regional to a national institution. It subsequently branched to many parts of Canada. By 1902 Eastern Townships Bank would have advanced $250,000 to Granby. As a consequence, a bank director would be a fixture on the Granby board. William Spier, who had been chief inspector for the bank, was assigned as manager of the Phoenix subagency. The 44th AR of the bank, June 3, 1903, sketches its expansion.

35. EMJ 70:5 (Aug. 4, 1900), 140. For further details, see Roy, "Railways, Politicians, and the Development of Vancouver" (thesis).

36. Hill to Shaughnessy, Aug. 3, 1901 (CPR). See Great Northern AR 1901: the Washington & Great Northern in Washington State and VV&E in British Columbia are "now building lines . . . from Marcus on the SF&N."

37. Sanford, *McCulloch's Wonder,* 35–50; *Phoenix Pioneer,* May 12, 1901, and April 30, 1904.

38. *SR* Nov. 10, 1899; EMJ 70:26 (Dec. 29, 1900), 770; Aldridge to Shaughnessy, Nov. 11, 1899 (CPR).

39. *Journal of the Canadian Mining Institute,* 1902, 171.

40. See BCM 1900, p. 769 and BCM 1901, p. 1052, for production by each mine for 1900 and 1901.

41. *Phoenix Pioneer,* June 30, Dec. 29, 1900, May 12, 1901; Graves to Shaughnessy, Dec. 3, 1901 (CPR).

42. Chapter 75, B.C. Legislature Laws 1901.

43. EMJ 71:25 (June 22, 1901), 814.

44. EMJ 72:21 (Nov. 23, 1901), 671, quoting *Canadian Mining Review,* Aug. 1901.

45. For Graves's liabilities, Graves to Shaughnessy, Dec. 30, 1901 (CPR). For Miner's views, EMJ, Nov. 23, 1901, 671.

46. Granby AR 1910, p. 24. West Kootenay Power and Light had absorbed Cascade Power, the original supplier to the smelter.

47. Graves to Shaughnessy, Dec. 3, Dec. 11, Dec. 17, Dec. 30, 1901, telegram, Aldridge to Graves, Dec. 16, 1901, and reply Dec. 17, 1901 (all CPR). Shaughnessy to Ledoux, Feb. 12, 1902 (S#76).

48. Graves to Hill, Oct. 3, 1902, written in St. Paul after conferring.

49. Ibid.

50. Graves to Hill, Oct. 18, 1902; Hill to E. T. Nichols, GN offices, New York, Oct. 23, 1902 (Hill).

CHAPTER 2: ONE OF THE BOYS

1. *Spokane Falls Review,* Jan. 1, March 17, 24, April 21, Dec. 24, 1887; Durham 1:378.

2. *SR* July 24, 1932; Jan. 19, 1948 (obit.); *Chr* Dec. 25, 1934. Spokane County deed indexes indicate that Frank Graves bought eight centrally located lots, and his wife, Maud, two between 1885 and 1887.

3. Gregg, *History of Hancock County,* 581; *Bounty Land Gazette* (Quincy, Ill.), Dec. 26, 1835; David Parker, Hancock County Historical Society, to author, March 9, 1987. Although in a family genealogy Reuben is said to be a founder of St. Mary's, he is not listed among those who platted it. Genealogy supplied by Janice Howe and Dorothy Phillips. Durham 3: 371–73, 421–23. Newspaper obituaries: Frank, *SR* Jan. 19, 1948; Jay, *SR* April 27, 1948; Carroll, *SR* May 14, 1929; William, *Chr* Feb. 15, 1945.

4. Spokane County deed index shows Clough and Graves bought parts of lots 1 and 2, block 1, Havermale's Addition; *Spokane Falls Review,* Dec. 24, 1887. Strahorn, "Ninety Years" (p. 256), describes Clough as "gently winning, not easily dismissed." Jay's father also came to Spokane in 1889 to live with Jay's half-sister, May Boydston, for whom Jay found a house: Spokane County deeds 115:386 (1901). The father died there in 1910. See obituary, *SR* Jan. 31, 1910.

5. Spokane *Times* quoted in Durham 1:412; *Spokane Falls Review,* March 24, 1887. Population data are from census reports for years indicated.

6. *Spokane Falls Review,* Jan. 1 and 20, 1887, Dec. 7, 1888 (mud), and Jan. 1, 1891.

7. Ibid., Jan. 3, 1891. Streetcars, Durham 1:413; park board minutes, June 1, 1908; Graves's house, 1417 Pacific (at Chestnut), a three-story frame now gone, was valued at $15,000. See Hook, *Spokane Falls* (pamphlet), 46.

8. See author's article, "When the Dutch Owned Spokane." In later

NOTES

years, Jay Graves clearly classed himself as one of Spokane's builders, remarking in an interview (*SR* April 7, 1914) that when he came to the city "the community was afflicted with a sort of commercial measles" and implying that his aggressive promotion, with the efforts of others, cured it. On the basis of other evidence, Graves's observation appears to discount the booster spirit evident in early Spokane.

9. Isaac C. Jolles to chairman, committee of Northwestern and Pacific stockholders, Aug. 15, 1896 (Hypotheekbank papers, EWSHS).

10. Author's review of deed records 1888–92; Durham 1:430, photo facing, shows tent.

11. *Spokane Falls Review,* May 29 and 30, July 11 and 30, 1890. Although a family tradition says Graves offered land for the college, no Graves site is among six considered by the Spokane Falls committee, and there is no record that Graves, at the time, owned the land north of Spokane he is supposed to have offered. A. O. Gray, *Not by Might,* 87, quotes Benjamin H. Kizer, late Spokane attorney, as saying Graves tried to bring the college to Spokane. Kizer, who joined Frank and Will Graves in their law firm in 1903, ought to know, but perhaps he, too, repeated a family myth. Graves did offer land for a Carnegie library in 1903, but another site was chosen.

12. Reavis, *City, passim; Spokane Review,* May 29, 1892.

13. Ads: *Spokane Falls Review,* April 20, 1890, Jan. 1, 1891; *Spokane Review,* Jan. 5, March 13, 1892.

14. "Average Age of Housing Units, 1961," map in Spokane City Plan Commission, *Needs and Resources,* 26. For best-selling additions based on construction values, *Spokane Falls Review,* Jan. 1, 1891. Developers also set the dimensions of lots, most 50 feet wide and 120 to 140 deep, but in some sections such as Nettleton's and Ide's on the north side, lots measured only 40 wide and 90 to 100 feet deep; Peaceful Valley lots were 25 feet wide, obviously intended for small houses. Interior residential lots throughout the city sold for about $300, corners about $400. Few contractors built on speculation early in this century.

15. See Mutschler, "Street Railway Development," *passim.* City directories usually described carline routes.

16. *Spokane Review,* April 29, 30, May 4, 5, 1892.

17. *Spokane Spokesman,* Dec. 18, 19, 1892; *Review,* Jan. 3, 1893.

18. See the author's "When the Dutch Owned Spokane." Some ledgers of the Dutch company are in the collection at EWSHS.

19. Based on author's review of county and title company deed records. Cook's losses are detailed in Spokane County civil case 8425 and deed book 75:43.

20. Northwestern and Pacific Hypotheekbank AR 1894 (EWSHS); *Spokane Review,* Jan. 6, 8, 1894, Jan. 1, 1895.

21. For discussions of these events, see the author's *Ballyhoo Bonanza,* 33–35, 56–59; *Inland Empire: D. C. Corbin and Spokane,* 145. Clark developed Arlington Heights; Grinnell, Columbia Addition.

22. This is SW¼ of Sec. 11, Township 25, Range 43 EWM. See Spokane County deeds 43:121, 49:42, and water right, Miscellaneous Records D:315. City ordinance A-325 purchases and condemns Clark's land and that abutting. *Spokane Review,* Dec. 12, 14, 1892.

23. *Spokane Review,* Jan. 5, 1893; mortgage, 7:197 and 71:415. This was the house later acquired by Sweeny, who would turn it over to Frank Graves in 1904 as partial payment for Glover's house. Graves resold it, deeds 144:315. *Dir* 1893 shows Fairweather and J. Graves at same address, 2107 Pacific.

24. City ordinance A-583 and attached documents, passed over mayor's veto; Theis and Barroll contract with contractor Rolla Jones, Jan. 10, 1894; Graves to council, June 4, 1895. Apparently a third bid, directly from Clark, was not considered. The city's authority to incur debt was in question, and many businessmen preferred a bond issue over warrants. See Winston v. Spokane, 12 Wash. 524 (1895), in which court rules that special fundings do not technically create indebtedness above the legal limit. In *Dir* 1893 Theis is listed as a resident of New York.

25. *SR* Jan. 1, 1897.

26. Jolles to chairman and stockholders of Hypotheekbank, Aug. 15, 1896 (EWSHS).

27. Unprocessed Adams business papers in Mass HS include the trust agreement and correspondence from the agents Hubbard and Sherwood. George Adams began buying in 1890, according to Spokane deed indexes, e.g., Booge to Adams 25:136; G. Adams to CFA2 55:420; Hubbard to B. Adams 55:105.

28. Based on author's review of deed records. For Clark and Sweeny, see author's *Ballyhoo Bonanza,* 134–38.

29. The City Beautiful movement is outlined in many accounts, e.g., author's "A. L. White, Champion of Urban Beauty," Olmsted, "Town-Planning Movement," Peterson, "City Beautiful Movement."

30. *SR* June 2, 5, 1897.

CHAPTER 3: SHAPING SPOKANE

1. *SR* May 6, 1900, reports that the American Mining Investment Co., Minneapolis, has optioned the Spokane and Montrose Electric Motor Railway Co. and with it, 60 acres; the company hopes to buy an additional 678 acres from the Hypotheekbank. Cook's transactions for Secs. 20 and 29, T25N, R43EWM, appear singly in Spokane County deed and mortgage records, perhaps best summarized in Spokane County civil suits 8425 and 10922, and record of sheriff's sales, 66:10, Feb. 16, 1895; 75:43, June 6, 1896. *SR* April 1, 1892, park; Feb. 10, 1918, F. Cook. These areas were platted as Manito Park, Cook's 1st through 4th, and Rockwood additions. Rockwood did not go to Graves's Spokane-Washington company.

2. *SR* May 12 and 13, 1903; "History of Properties" (GN 9128); Spokane Traction Co. articles of incorporation name as trustees J. P. Graves, Clyde Graves, Fred Grinnell, C. Reeder, and A. White. Reeder, as Spokane manager of Provident Trust, represented bondholders.

3. *SR* Jan. 9, 1916 quotation; Nov. 29 and 30, 1899.

4. WWP AR 1901, p. 6; AR 1902, pp. 6–7. The classic study of the relationship between trolleys and real estate development is Warner, *Streetcar Suburbs*; see also Friedricks, "Henry E. Huntington and Real Estate Development in Southern California."

5. *Spokane Blue Book, 1902–03*.

6. Spokane-Washington Improvement Co., articles of incorporation, Spokane County 76142, Feb. 25, 1903. The directors were Jay Graves, Will Graves, David Ham, Fred Grinnell, and Aaron Kuhn, the last a banker. *SR* March 8, 1904. The club's ground is depicted in a pamphlet, "Manito Park—from Teepee to Mansion" (EWSHS). After its clubhouse burned, the club proposed to move to an area near Fort Wright, then did move briefly to quarters near Liberty Park, until Graves offered a site on the Little Spokane River, which it now occupies. *SR* Nov. 3, 1908; *Spokane Press*, Nov. 23, 1909.

7. *SR* Sept. 15, 25, 1903; Spokane Park Board *AR,* June 1, 1908; park board minutes, April 27, June 7, 1910. Manito Park comprises portions of Manito Park, South Side Cable, and Cook's 3d additions, and unplatted land donated by Frank Hogan. According to *SR* Sept. 15, 1903, Cook planned two 40-acre parks in much the same location. One of Graves's managers, a former city councilman, Henry M. Lillienthal, took the contract to build the drive; he became entangled in broken promises and paid for the work from his own pocket, battling the city to compensate him.

8. "Manito Park—from Teepee to Mansion"; the description of Grin-

nell is from Strahorn, "90 Years," 256. The city council approved the plat Feb. 28, 1905.

9. Deed 117208, 163:313; conversation with Joel E. Ferris II.

10. JCO to White, March 17, 1909, quoting a 1906 letter (LC); *Dictionary of American Biography*, s.v. "Olmsted, John C." Various letters in Olmsted papers show White's participation in Olmsted's visits to Spokane.

11. Quotations from a 1908 outline of a city plan published in 1913 as *Report of the Board of Park Commissioners, 1891–1913*, 71–97. It is clear, however, from correspondence that the plan was forming in White's and Olmsted's minds well before 1908. Trees: *Chr* Aug. 16, 1905. For an extended discussion of White's park work, see author's "A. L. White, Champion of Urban Beauty."

12. C. F. Adams's children were John II, Charles II, Henry, Brooks, and Mary. The Adams Real Estate Trust was set up in 1887 to manage real estate bequeathed to them. Their principal agent was Charles J. Hubbard, Kansas City, who worked through Sherwood to buy and manage properties in Spokane. An inventory of ARET holdings, Jan. 1, 1908, Mass HS, lists Spokane properties.

13. The discussion is based in part on Nagel, "West That Failed," on Adams business papers (Mass HS), and on Spokane County deed records. Hubbard to CFA2, Sept. 17, 1889, has manuscript notations showing the first purchase was authorized Sept. 21, 1889. *SR* May 1, 1900, reports a visit to Spokane by CFA2 and quotes him as saying, "I make this country part of my routine every year." His sons worked on his ranch near Lewiston, Idaho.

14. *SR* Nov. 4, 1902, May 25, 1904, Feb. 5, 1905; A. Beamer to C. Leavy, Feb. 25, 1905 (NP Pres. 1304). The author found no indication in Adams papers that CFA2 invested in a railway through Moran Prairie. Mark Mendenhall, a developer, was president, and Sherwood, vice-president. The Moran promoters considered beginning with an 8-mile line in 1905 but postponed construction (MS 38, 14/182, EWSHS).

15. *SR* Feb. 11, 1905, quotation; Feb. 12, 1905; Oct. 29 and 30, 1908, Hogan. Hogan's purchases are in Sherwood Addition.

16. WWP, Statement A, 32–35; WWP AR 1909, *passim*. Corporate data on S&IE from NP Pres. 1604-2. According to this source, only $634,000 of the issue was used, and in 1906, with merger, the bonds became an obligation of the consolidated S&IE. Part of the stock issue was applied to a one-third interest in the Terminal Co. Directors of the Traction Co. in 1905: Graves, Clark, Thomas Greenough, White, and Grinnell. *Chr*

NOTES 113

June 14, 1905. Graves was also bidding, with Robert Strahorn, to purchase the Spokane gas company.

17. *SR* Jan. 22, 1905 (4th ward); *Chr* Jan. 11, 1906 (Manito); Colborn, in Durham 3:182–84, gives his version of his role in developing Manito Park; JCO notes, May 13, 1908 (LC) remark on relationship between White and Mauzey, whom White hoped to enlist in his park movement.

18. *Chr* Aug. 28, 1908; *SR* March 31, 1907 (White City); Oct. 4, 1908, on sale of Graves's interest.

19. *Chr* Aug. 28, 1908 (fairgrounds route); a map is in the corporation counsel's file 1656(3/3) among Spokane city records at EWU; *SR* March 16, 1904; Sept. 24, 1908. An editorial, *SR* Sept. 25, 1908, observes: "Even 5 mills a car mile would be considered . . . a low figure." Many routes are detailed by Mutschler, "Street Railway Development in Spokane." A detailed description of WWP equipment may be found in ERJ 34:14 (Oct. 2, 1909), 524–28.

20. *SR* Oct. 15 and 19, 1905. WWP claimed it paid $20,000 for use of the bridge. Richards to W. A. White, Chairman of finance committee, a Brooklyn broker, Nov. 1, 1905 (WWP Box 31, WSU).

21. *SR* June 28, 1905; JCO notes, Oct. 26, Nov. 5, Nov. 6, and Nov. 14, 1908 (LC) on boulevard plans; Richards to Elliott, Oct. 10, 1910 (NP Pres. 1603). W. A. White also approached the Northern Pacific to join WWP in building suburban railways to compete with Graves. He discusses this in a letter to Richards, Aug. 8, 1906 (WWP Box 32, WSU).

22. WWP ARs 1911 and 1914; route maps, Spokane corporation counsel file 1656(3/3) (EWU).

23. Lee et al., *Population Redistribution,* Vol. 1, table P-1, p. 220; WWP AR 1904, quotation. Permits from *Dirs* 1903, 1908, 1909, Durham 1:547, and *SR* Jan. 10, 1910. Building records prior to 1910 were destroyed in a fire.

24. Spokane Water Department, *First Annual Report,* 1911, especially pp. 13, 21, 27, 29–30, 33, and 47; Spokane *Official Gazette,* Aug. 18, 1913, p. 2331, records the purchase of one of these private water systems; Ordinance C441, 1911, refunding water bonds; *SR* Feb. 11, 1905, quotes Emeline Sweeny.

25. *Report of the Board of Park Commissioners,* 7; park board minutes, May 20 and 25, 1907.

26. JCO notes, March 28 and 30, 1907(LC); Brown: *SR* April 16, 1933 and Dec. 10, 1951; Adams transfer to Brown, Dec. 1, 1911, Spokane County deeds grantee index; see platbooks. Rockwood is a comparatively small

addition between Fourteenth and Seventeenth bounded by Hatch and Arthur streets, and the area popularly called Rockwood is Graves's Manito Park 2d. What was to be Highland Boulevard is Rockwood Boulevard because the Highland name had been taken.

27. Sherwood to Hubbard, Sept. 29, 1893, forwarded to John Adams, Oct. 4, 1893 (Mass HS); Spokane v. NP Railway et al., ICC Opinion 820 (Feb. 9, 1909); Sen. C. F. Manderson, Nebr., to Adams, Jan. 18, 1895, and Sen. J. R. Hawley, Conn., to Adams, Jan. 27, 1895 (Mass HS).

28. JCO notes March 28, 30, and June 18, 1907; March 27, May 22, 25, 1909; Feb. 1, May 1, 1910 (all LC). *SR* Sept. 25, 1910, featured sketches of Rockwood homes.

29. JCO notes, Nov. 19, 1908 (LC); park board minutes, Nov. 27, 1907, and Dec. 30, 1908.

30. *SR* Oct. 28, 1909; May 21, 1911; and Dec. 28, 1913; JCO notes, May 7, 1910, mentions improvements to area, and May 12, 1910, stores (LC). *SR* Jan. 7, 1910, reports a sale of four and one-half acres on Rockwood for "about $10,000 an acre," breaking "all records for sensational prices on residence property in Spokane." The newspaper describes Rockwood as "a colony for rare homes, costing from $50,000 to $200,000 each." Rockwood was selling, at the time, at an average of $8,000 an acre, highest in Spokane's history to then. Cannon Hill rose to roughly $2,000 an acre. By contrast, A. B. Campbell had paid $9,000 for six lots in Browne's Second Addition in 1898 and built a mansion there for $25,000.

31. *SR* Feb. 26, 1909; Malloy Brothers to Sherwood, Nov. 14, 1908, and Sherwood to CFA2, Nov. 14, 1908; Sherwood to CFA2, Jan. 15, 1909, enclosing option agreement. The agreement gave the Malloys 40 days to analyze their project for a payment of $1,000 (Mass HS).

32. *SR* Oct. 11, 1910; letterhead, Boulevard Park Realty Co., Nov. 4, 1912 (LC); for Glasgow, see Durham 2:241–42. Boulevard Park Co. articles of incorporation, Spokane County No. 233387, March 15, 1909; amended, No. 254437, Nov. 15, 1909, to increase capital stock and name Glasgow and others as directors.

33. *SR* Jan. 15, 17, 1909.

34. Adams sold Lincoln Heights for $367,000, which enabled him to pay off the $165,000 loan from Adams Trust secured by the property. Release of mortgage March 15, 1909. Spokane County 186:418; plat filed March 30, 1909. JCO notes on a visit with Kiernan and Lawyer, May 25, 1909 (LC). *SR* Jan. 12, 15, 1909.

35. Lawyer's property, deed 150035, 182:150, 182:152; JCO notes, May 25, June 19, 1909 (LC).

NOTES 115

36. Spokane Water Department *First Annual Report, passim; SR* Jan. 15, 1910; June 28, 1911.

37. JCO notes, May 25, 1909, quotations; May 11, 12, 1910 (LC).

38. *SR* Jan. 17, 1909 (quotation), Oct. 21, 1909, March 27, 1910.

39. Will Graves quoted, *SR* Sept. 22, 1908.

40. Richards to Elliott, Oct. 13, 1910, and reply Oct. 18, 1910; Elliott to Graves, Oct. 18, 1910; Graves to Elliott, Oct. 21, 1910 (NP Pres. 1603).

41. WWP AR 1912 on autos and AR 1921 on summary of patronage; Waldo Paine to Budd, chief engineer, GN, Feb. 28, 1913 (NP 1375).

42. *Chr* June 6, 1918; *SR* June 9, 30, 1918. Shuff to Dawson, Sept. 10, 1915, to JCO Jan. 19, 1918, to Olmsted Brothers, Jan. 31, 1921 (LC); Sherwood to CFA2, 13, 1918 (Mass HS).

43. *SR* Jan. 22, 1911; April 12, 1925.

CHAPTER 4: THE ELECTRIC RAILWAY

1. *SR* Oct. 22, 1902, mentions agitation over "poor service by NP"; Nov. 16, 1902, says farmers who sold Blackwell right-of-way demanded assurance that his road was not controlled by OR&N; John Finch confided that Graves and Blackwell approached him together in May 1903 to subscribe to the Coeur d'Alene line (H. Richards to C. Mellen, May 14, 1903, NP Pres. 972). Blackwell obituary, *Newport (Wash.) Miner*, Dec. 14, 1922, characterizes him as "quiet, unassuming . . . [a man who] never liked the limelight." Articles of incorporation: Poor's RR 1905, pp. 1160–61, gives incorporation date as March 12, 1903, the date of filing; Coeur d'Alene & Spokane Ry, articles No. 89, Kootenai County, Idaho, Oct. 21, 1902. Judging from correspondence with Hill, Graves contemplated an electric interurban in 1901.

2. J. M. Hannaford to Mellen, June 5, 1903; T. Cooper to Mellen, June 8, 1903; H. M. Stephens to Cooper, June 27, 1903; B. E. Palmer, division engineer, to W. L. Darling, NP chief engineer, Dec. 27, 1902 (all NP Pres. 972); L. W. Hill to D. Lamont, April 26, 1905 (NP Pres. 1375). Louis Hill tried for some time to persuade his father to break off with Graves, as evidenced by a letter in WWP files, H. R. Richards to W. A. White, July 29, 1908 (WWP Box 33, WSU), to the effect that Louis "impressed his father with his opinion of Graves" and the elder Hill "has made up his mind to sever connections."

3. Mellen to W. Clough, NP chairman, July 10, 1903 (NP Pres. 972); *Railway and Engineering Review*, Feb. 9, 1907, 102. Hill could not stand Mellen, who was soon succeeded by Howard Elliott.

4. *Railway Age,* Nov. 11, 1904; Spokane Traction, amended articles, July 22, 1905; Elliott to R. Bacon, June 10, 1905; Levey to Elliott, March 18, 1905, quotation, and April 30, 1906, enclosing C&S statements (both NP Pres. 972); Hill to E. D. Adams, March 28, 1898, pointing out he will not forfeit access to the Palouse (Hill, book P-16, roll 11, p. 289.) Graves talked of extending his electric railway into the Big Bend, that dry agricultural country embraced by the Columbia River in the elbow west of Spokane, now generally called by its geographic designation, the Columbia Plateau, or, since the advent of federal irrigation, the Columbia Basin. *SR* Nov. 7, 1908, quotes Graves as declaring he has secured half the right-of-way for an extension between Davenport and Peach, a town on the Columbia River. Graves also considered building a power station at Little Falls on the Spokane River. See author's article, "Power Plays: The Enigma of Little Falls," *Pacific Northwest Quarterly* 82:4 (Oct. 1991), 122–31.

5. McClaine to F. P. Kane, U.S. deputy comptroller, Nov. 6, 1908, answering allegation that he lent one borrower more than the legal limit (NA).

6. Elliott to Bacon, June 10, 1905 (NP Pres. 1340) mentions Higginson. The Higginson letterbooks at the Baker Library, Harvard University, do not reveal correspondence with Graves. Higginson was a member of the Union Pacific reorganization committee and could be expected to resist a new railroad into the Palouse.

7. Hannaford to Elliott, June 23, 1905 (NP Pres. 1340), reporting his conversation with Ristine. Hilton and Due, *Electric Interurban Railways in America,* 25–27, 30 and 36 (they quote Alfred M. Lamar on investments); *Railway Age,* Dec. 20, 1907, p. 895, on Oregon Lines; Van Deusen, "Electric Interurban Railway Bonds as Investments," 338, quotation. Van Deusen gives a rule of thumb for construction costs and population served, as a guide for investment in suburban routes. In general, he agreed with other analysts that well-positioned and -managed electrics offered good possibilities for profitable investment. "Prosperous Trolleys," in *Review of Reviews,* May 1908, points out that lines serving large populations and diverse businesses produced 2.65% increased income for bondholders between 1907 and 1908. "Electric Railway Developments," *Scientific American Supplement 1606* (Oct. 13, 1906) remarks that "during the past ten years the electric railway business has developed far more rapidly than any other of comparable size" (p. 25738). These are examples of thoughtful reviews of electric lines that encouraged investment.

8. Luke D. Wolford in *Colfax Commoner,* July 17, 1891. It should be noted that the Union Pacific and subsidiaries were oriented to Portland and to building up Oregon.

9. Articles of incorporation (Spokane County 128600), amended July 12, 21, and 23, 1906; Jones ad, *SR* Jan. 6, 1907; Grinnell ad folder, EWSHS "business" file.

10. *Colfax Commoner* quoting *Pullman Tribune* with comment, Jan. 20, 1905; *SR* Aug. 31, 1905; June 23, 1907.

11. *Chr* Jan. 13, Feb. 2, 1905; *Colfax Commoner,* March 24, 1905. F. J. Pearson, NP chief engineer, to Elliott and others, April 26, 1905; Mitchell to Hannaford, March 31, 1905 (NP Pres. 1340). For Waverly sugar plant, see author's *Inland Empire: D. C. Corbin and Spokane,* 198–201.

12. *Railway Age,* March 9, 1906, p. 363; March 30, 1906, p. 598; July 26, 1907, pp. 133–34. *ERJ* Nov. 21, 1908, p. 1423, gives statistics of single-phase railways in North America. The Coeur d'Alene road remained a three-phase system operating on 600 volts direct current.

13. The description of the system has been simplified. It is based on a report, "Transmission Lines," of the S&IE (GN 9128, 19.E.1.7B, Minn HS) and *Railway Age,* Feb. 9, 1907, pp. 103–104. The Graves road is said to have purchased its cars from J. G. Brill and American Car and Foundry. The frequency-changing station was designed by the Spokane architect Albert Held.

14. *Chr* Jan. 2, 1904; Blackwell Park Addition, Kootenai County platbook B:139, Aug. 15, 1907; Liberty Lake Land Co., articles of incorporation, June 8, 1907 (Spokane County 175106); a pamphlet advertising Wicomico is in EWSHS (quotation); Hayden Lake Improvement Co., articles, June 12, 1906 (GN Pres. 9128); W. F. Turner, comptroller, SP&S, to Hannaford, June 17, 1915, summarizing S&IE corporate data (NP Pres. 1604-2). For his Coeur d'Alene park, Blackwell apparently appropriated the best lands of old Fort Sherman. In a letter to Sen. W. B. Heyburn, March 13, 1903, urging the senator to hurry the Department of Interior's approval of the C&S right-of-way, D. H. Budlong, register of the Coeur d'Alene land office, objected that the railroad took all the fort lands that did not overflow in high water, "the only high and dry land along the whole lakefront of the [fort] reservation." His protest went unheeded. (Railroads, General Land Office, RG 49, Div. F[I], Box 68, NA).

15. Charles E. Flagg, called an "advertising agent"; see ERJ 32:19c (Oct. 15, 1908), 1085–87; *SR* Dec. 17, 1906. Stations: ERJ 32:24 (Nov. 14, 1908), 1372; *Colfax Commoner,* March 30, 1906. Quotation from ERJ 32: 190 (Oct. 16, 1908), 1128.

16. Elliott to J. N. Hill, NP vice-president, Sept. 14, 1906 (NP Pres. 1340). *SR* Nov. 7, 1908, quotes Graves as saying his Spokane, Columbia & Western Railroad (his Big Bend road) has purchased half of the right-of-

way needed between the towns of Davenport and Peach, the latter on the Columbia River. Among the line's directors were officers of the Portland & Seattle (later, Spokane, Portland & Seattle), a joint enterprise of the Northern Pacific and Great Northern. An open amalgamation of Graves and Hill interests, the proposed Spokane, Columbia & Western surveyed from Spokane to the juncture of the Spokane and Columbia rivers and thence north to Peach. Its 30,000 shares were subscribed but never issued, and the company built no track. It was one of several proposed roads whose managers said they would build dams in the Spokane River. See the author's "Power Plays: The Engima of Little Falls." A tentative route for the Graves road was surveyed by Clarence H. Stewart in 1908. Stewart's notes on the costs of maintaining the surveying party are among the Stewart papers, Minn HS.

17. Notes reported at special S&IE trustees' meeting, Dec. 15, 1906 (NP 1340-M); Coeur d'Alene: Levey to Elliott, April 30, 1906 (NP Pres. 972).

18. Stockholders approved consolidation Nov. 9, 1906, but the actual conveyances of subsidiary properties varied: Terminal Co., Nov. 27, 1906; S&IE and Traction Co., Feb. 13, Coeur d'Alene & Spokane, Feb. 12, 1908. The resorts, power sites, and real estate companies continued as separate entities. The Spokane & Inland was dissolved June 21, 1909.

19. S&IE Minutes, Jan. 19, 1906 (NP 1340-M).

20. The issue of "rights" arose in a suit against the railroad: Johnston v. S&IE and Grinnell, Washington Supreme Court 14676, transcript furnished by Commissioner Goeffrey Crooks; 104 Wash. 562, 177 Pac. 810 (1919). See also Poor's RR 1909, p. 1300. According to a summary in 1915 by the SP&S comptroller, the S&IE issued 64,091 preferred rights (NP Pres. 1604-2). Differences between Graves and Blackwell had been evident for some time, witness a letter in WWP files, Richards to White, Dec. 6, 1904 (WWP Box 31, WSU): "I am told by Mr. [Robert] Rutter that he [Blackwell] is heartily sick of Graves and would be glad to sever his connection with him if he could."

21. Graves to Hill, April 6, 1906 (Hill). The Graves brothers sold small amounts of stock to some owners of Granby by giving common to those who bought preferred rights. Preferred sold at less than par, going at an average of $52. Among the Spokane buyers were Will Graves's crony, Moses Oppenheimer, 750 rights; Maud (Mrs. Frank) Graves, 350; and smaller buyers including C. D. Bibbins, J. M. Comstock, George R. Dodson, William J. Nicholls (stockbroker), and Julius Galland.

22. *Chr* Feb. 22, 1907; the Washington State Railroad Commission estimated Hill's holdings at 21,000 shares, according to *SR* Oct. 29, 1909,

which seems accurate; memo agreement of the Lake Superior Co., Ltd., 1899, in Hill files, furnished by W. Thomas White, curator. The company was organized under Sec. 2365, Laws of Michigan 1877, and managed by James J. Hill, James N. Hill, an NP vice-president, and R. I. Farrington. S&IE stockholders' minutes, June 15, 1906, list voting shares.

23. Prospectus Nov. 10, 1906 (NP Pres. 1340); 5 percent gold coupon bonds dated May 1, 1906, in $1,000 denominations, priced at par, to be retired 1911–25 by a sinking fund. In his letter, Graves mentions the Spokane Power Development Co. as a subsidiary to build the railroad's hydroelectric stations, but this company never merged into the S&IE. For a time, Graves was associated with David Wilson, a promoter, in a plan to develop the generating site at Little Falls on the Spokane River, and he arranged with Rep. Wesley L. Jones for passage of a bill in Congress (March 3, 1905, 33 Stats. 1006) providing for acquisition of water rights along the southern boundary of the Spokane Indian Reservation. WWP purchased Wilson's interest and built a dam and powerhouse at Little Falls 1908–10.

24. *Railway and Engineering Review,* Feb. 9, 1907, pp. 103–05; *Colfax Commoner,* April 12, 1907; S&IE trustees' special meeting, April 26, 1906 (NP 1340-M); *Chr* Sept. 28, 1905, and Feb. 24, 1906.

25. Graves to Hill, Oct. 3, 1906 (Hill) recapitulating a conversation in Spokane.

26. See ERJ 32:19 (Oct. 10, 1909), 898–902, and *SR* Jan. 13, 1907, sec. 3 for detailed descriptions of the Nine Mile plant. Spokane franchise A-1329, March 31, 1903, expiring in 1945. Secondary power sales: J. H. Young to C. R. Gray, SP&S, and Elliott, June 7, 1913 (NP Pres. 1340-D). The largest customer was the Inland Empire Paper Co. According to a letter in author's possession, Thomas Brewer, Exchange National Bank, to Harry L. Day, Aug. 20, 1909, J. P. Graves and A. L. White agreed to put $50,000–$75,000 into the paper company.

27. *Chr* March 11, 1906 (Kettle Falls); "Transmission Lines and Power Plant Sites" of S&IE (GN 9128). Hogan was president of the Spokane Light and Power Co. with offices in Frank Graves's suite in the Fernwell. The company did not function.

28. Annual report in ERJ 32:19 (Oct. 10, 1908), 935; dividends: S&IE trustees' minutes, Dec. 1, 1906, March 22, June 24, and Oct. 1, 1907 (all NP 1340-M); C. W. Bunn to Hannaford, April 4, 1917, analyzing S&IE finances (NP Pres. 1604-2).

29. S&IE Trustees' minutes, April 8, May 13, Aug. 31, Sept. 10, Nov. 11, 1907; June 8, 1908 (all NP 1340-M).

30. S&IE Trustees' minutes Nov. 8, 1908; Jan. 11, 16, and 25, 1909 (all NP 1340-M). Graves had contemplated a tunnel for part of his approach to the terminal but dropped this plan and placed on the market the land reserved for a tunnel route. See *SR* Nov. 13, 1908.

31. Elliott to White, Feb. 1, 1909 (NP Pres. 1340).

32. Train use based on descriptions in ERJ 33:17 (April 24, 1909), 790–91; 36:19 (Oct. 8, 1910), 633–36; *Chr* Sept. 8, 9, and 26, 1909; *SR* Oct. 29, 1909. Clyde Graves's memo on courtesy: ERJ 33:10 (March 6, 1909), 442. Quotation in ERJ 34:21 (Nov. 27, 1909), 1089–90, from an editorial that says 1908 freight equaled 25.6 percent of S&IE operating revenue. Paine to Elliott, March 28, 1911, reports Potlatch traffic (NP Pres. 1375).

33. *SR* Aug. 1 and 2, 1909.

34. *SR* Aug. 2, 1909 (editorial quotation); April 19, 1910; June 13, 1916; damage total, transcript, Johnston v. S&IE and Grinnell, Washington Supreme Court 14676; book costs of construction appear in "History of Properties . . . S&IE Railroad Co." (GN 9128); annual report, ERJ 34:21 (Nov. 27, 1909), 1116.

35. Shares based on holdings reported at stockholders' meetings (NP 1340-M); *SR* Oct. 29, 1909.

36. Capital stock: C. W. Bunn analysis to Hannaford, April 4, 1917 (NP Pres. 1604-2); notes, S&IE trustees' meeting, Aug. 10, 1910 (NP 1340-M). The Milwaukee speculation appeared in *SR* Oct. 29, 1909, and was copied by a number of newspapers.

37. *SR* Oct. 29, 30, and 31 (quotation), 1909.

38. "Frenzied Finance in Spokane," *Mining Truth,* March 3, 1919.

39. S&IE trustees' minutes, Aug. 10, 1910 (NP 1340-M); Clyde Graves to Elliott, Jan. 31, 1910; Elliott to G. T. Slade, third vice-president, NP, Feb. 9 and March 10, 1910; to C. Graves, March 17, 1910; J. P. Graves to Elliott, Dec. 8, 1910 (NP Pres. 1603); Elliott to J. P. Graves, Dec. 8, 1910 (except as noted, all NP Pres. 1340).

40. Elliott and L. W. Hill to Graves, April 19, 1911; Elliott to Gray, June 8, 1911 (NP Pres. 1375).

41. Elliott to J. N. Hill, April 30, 1911; L. W. Hill to Graves, June 8, 1911 (NP Pres. 1604); ERJ 38:4 (July 22, 1911), 176; Gray to L. W. Hill and Elliott, June 24, 1911 (NP Pres. 1604); special S&IE trustees' meeting minutes, June 24, 1911 (NP 1340-M). S&IE trustees' minutes, Sept. 16, 1912 (NP 1340-M) show Westinghouse arrears. Gray and Coolidge divided their time between the S&IE and SP&S.

42. Gray to Elliott, June 17, 1911 (NP Pres. 1604).

43. Gilman to Clough, June 9, 1915 (NP Pres. 1604-2).

44. F. Elliott to H. Elliott, Nov. 29, 1918 (NP 1340-M).

45. Hannaford to H. Elliott, June 4, 1918 (NP Pres. 1604-2). A chart of S&IE subsidiaries and tracklaying dates by Clyde Parent in EWSHS sets Sept. 30, 1941, as "the last electric service." Hidy and Hidy, *Great Northern*, attempt a chronology of the S&IE, 320–22, in substantial agreement with Parent. Their data do not wholly agree with dates in S&IE files, Minn HS.

46. S&IE was acquired by the Spokane & Eastern Railway Jan. 10, 1919, and the Spokane & Eastern became the Spokane, Coeur d'Alene & Palouse on May 2, 1927, according to WWP files.

47. Last trains: *Chr* March 20, 1939; *SR* July 14, 1940; a photo by Clyde Parent, in the files of the Inland Empire Railway Historical Society, shows a Spokane, Coeur d'Alene & Palouse train, pulled by an electric locomotive with pantograph, departing for Moscow on March 28, 1939. WWP records show that the utility acquired the Hayden Lake distribution system Jan. 21, 1930.

CHAPTER 5: GRANBY

1. Nichols: *NYT* Feb. 23, 1930; *National Cyclopedia of American Biography*, 24:285–86; *GFG* Sept. 14, 1903. Stanton: *NYT* Feb. 24, 1906; Benedict, *Red Metal*, 112–13; *Who Was Who* 1:1171.

2. *GFG* Sept. 14 and Oct. 17, 1903. Sussman had earlier reviewed Boundary for the Canadian Pacific.

3. Quoted in *GFG* March 28, 1903.

4. O. B. Smith to Graves, July 15, 1910, in AR 1910, pp. 9–18 (quotation, 10). For geology of Boundary, see LeRoy, *Geology and Ore Deposits*, passim, esp. 79–80.

5. Shaughnessy to William Whyte, June 20, 1904 (S#84); Hill to A. D. Cartwright, secretary, Board of Railway Commissioners, Jan. 6, 1916 (Hill letterbook P22); "of superior quality," GN AR 1901, p. 12. Eagle, *Canadian Pacific Railroad and . . . Western Canada*, 246–48, sketches the CPR's coal interests. If Hill and Shaughnessy agreed on nothing else, their views of Lindsey coincided.

6. Shaughnessy to Graves, Oct. 31, 1902 (S#79), to Whyte, July 7, 1902 (S#78), to F. L. Underwood, B.C. Copper, Dec. 29, 1902 (S#79), to Aldridge, Dec. 6, 1903 (S#83).

7. *Toronto Daily News*, April 8, 1904. Hill was said to have bought 34,000 shares of 100,000 at a premium of 60 percent above market price;

see *Mining and Engineering Record,* July 27, 1917, p. 190; BCM 1902, p. 1071; Shaughnessy to J. W. Ellsworth, Nov. 23, 1903 (S#83). Rexford, Montana, was the shipping station until the Great Northern realigned its main line.

8. EMJ 72:16 (Oct. 19, 1901), 523; Spokane County articles of incorporation No. 62967, April 28, 1902; *Inland Sentinel* (Kamloops), July 28, 1903, quoting *GFG;* Hill to Cox, Nov. 8, 1902 (Hill letterbook P18). Clippings on International may be found in GAIA (M1561) f. 334.

9. Shaughnessy to Whyte, July 4, 1904 (S#84), to executive agent, Vancouver, Aug. 1, 1901 (S#74).

10. Turner, *West of the Great Divide,* 130; Railway Committee order Oct. 20, 1902 (PAC RG43, AII1, vol. 126); report Jan. 5, 1904, by William McCarthy, inspecting engineer, to Chief Engineer, Dept. of Railways and Canals, and March 9, 1905 (PAC RG43 vol. 231); Railway Branch, Dept. of Railways and Canals, to J. H. Kennedy, VV&E chief engineer, Feb. 10, 1904 (PAC RG43 vol. 126).

11. *GFG* Oct. 8 and 22, 1904; Baillie, "Half-Century of Mining," 8.

12. *GFG* Oct. 8, 1904. Higginson especially, of this group, had profited from the Calumet and Hecla, a bountiful Michigan copper mine. The Hill Reference Library collection contains a few letters from Hill to members of this board, e.g., to Clark, Feb. 21, 1905, indicating Hill's personal involvement in Granby.

13. Shaughnessy to Whyte, July 25, 1904 (S#84); BCM 1904, G 221.

14. Shaughnessy to Hon. Charles Fitzpatrick, Feb. 7, 1905 (S#86); *Railway Age,* 44:2 (July 12, 1907), 35–36.

15. Shaughnessy to Flumerfelt, April 1, 1902 (S#77); PABC Cominco file (MMS 15) showing shipments 1902–10 and 1914 by mine and railroad; Ballie, "Half-Century of Mining," 9.

16. *GFG* Sept. 30, 1905; Seattle *Post-Intelligencer,* Sept. 30, 1905.

17. Baillie, "Half-Century of Mining," 11; Granby AR 1910, esp. "Comparative Tonnage Statement," 25; *Mines Handbook 1918,* p. 1492, shows dividends 1903–17; Poor's Industrials, 1917, pp. 282–83; *GFG* Dec. 17, 1904.

18. Campbell, "Granby Mines," 162, 164, 170. Poor's Industrials, 1915, p. 1164.

19. Herfindal, *Copper Costs,* 84 and 85 n. 3, table 21, p. 203; Herfindal also discusses collusion; U.S. Federal Trade Commission, *Report on the Copper Industry,* 244; Ledoux quoted in *GFG* Sept. 14, 1903, a reprint of his 1902 report; costs exclusive of marketing, Granby AR 1910, p. 25 (for fiscal years ending June 30); dividends reported in Poor's Industrials, 1915, p. 1164. *Mines Handbook 1918,* p. 1492, gives a higher figure for 1908. Poor's total, however, agrees with Graves's in AR 1910, p. 8.

20. *GFG* Nov. 18, 1905; *NYT* Jan. 24, 1907.

21. Crow's Nest Pass Coal Co. minutes, Jan. 17, 1906, and Feb. 21, 1906 (GAIA M1561, vol. 5); *Chicago Post,* Aug. 19, 1905, gives a highly colored account of Hill's buy; Hill to E. T. Nichols, Jan. 10, 1908 (Hill letterbook P19); under the CPR's agreement with Crow's Nest, it could not mine coal in the pass until January 1909, when it began using the Hosmer site. The figure 52 percent is Hill's in a letter to Graves, May 21, 1907 (Hill letterbook P19). Hill's stock was in the name of the Northern Securities Co. A stockholders list Sept. 18, 1907 (GAIA M1516, f. 628) shows Graves with 25, Granby with 3,000 shares. On this list, Gault's name is lined out, and Granby's penciled in. (Some accounts say Graves bought 8,000 for Granby.) A column showing proportions has Granby 405, Graves 16.66, which would make Hill's 2,561, and that fits with the 45 percent he was said to have bought earlier. A later list, showing Granby with 5,675 and Graves with 41 shares, is evidently the stock basis on which Hill forced changes in the directorate.

22. Hill to Cox, July 25, 1907 (Hill letterbook P19); Crow's Nest minutes, Jan. 15, 1908 (GAIA M1561, vol. 5), 193; *GFG,* Dec. 28, 1907 (quotation).

23. Hodges to J. E. McAllister, B.C. Copper, July 14, 1909; McAllister to Newman Erb, president, Dec. 17, 1909 (both in Mine, Mill and Smelter Workers, University of British Columbia, 147-1).

24. *GFG* April 4, 1908, and Oct. 29, 1910 (quotation); *Granby News* 3:10 (Oct. 1919); *Canadian Mining Journal,* 31:22 (Nov. 15, 1910), 681; EMJ 91:24 (June 17, 1911), 1193. Rodgers was a familiar figure in Boundary and other western mining camps.

25. *SR* March 25, 1910 (stock and Graves quotation); *Canadian Mining Journal* 31:9 (May 1, 1910), 259–60 and 269; *NYT* March 26 and Oct. 5, 1910; *GFG* March 31, 1910, reports that 3,500 shares were traded when the bad news broke.

26. EMJ 89:14 (April 2, 1910), 692.

27. *NYT* March 25 and Oct. 5, 1910; Sussman, Granby AR 1910, 15.

28. EMJ 90:15 (Oct. 8, 1910), 699–700; *NYT* Oct. 5, 1910 (quotation). In his letter to James Hill, Nov. 19, 1913 (Hill), Graves remarks that "George Clark disposed of his interest because of my demanding the resignation of his son . . . on account of the report which he joined in making with Mr. Langeloth."

29. *GFG* Oct. 8, 1913.

30. Graves to Hill, Nov. 19, 1913 (Hill). Graves and White bought back into Granby after the 1910 market fall. In his letter, Graves tells Hill he

owns 3,000 shares outright and 1,000 "owed for." White, in a letter to J. F. Dawson, Jan. 3, 1913, remarks that he has "picked up considerable Granby" recently (LC).

31. Zapata Corp., proxy statement, Nov. 13, 1978; *Western Miner,* June 1974. To acquire Copper Mountain, Granby increased its capital stock from 250,000 to 500,000 shares, using 155,000 to pay Canada Copper Corp. EMJ Oct. 14, 1916, p. 727; *Mining Age* quoted in *GFG* Oct. 18, 1913.

CHAPTER 6: CHANGING FORTUNES

1. Olmsted plan, April 7, 1910 (LC); *SR* Nov. 7, 1909.
2. JCO notes April 28 and 30, 1910 (LC); *SR* Jan. 3, 1909.
3. L. C. Gilman to Hannaford and R. Budd, July 6, 1914 (quotations), and Hannaford to Gilman, July 20, 1914 (NP Pres. 6696).
4. The Spokane Club building, designed by Cutter and Malmgren, was completed in 1911; it is among the buildings designated the Riverside Avenue Historical District in the National Register of Historic Places.
5. 117 Wash. 587 (1921). This is an appeal to the state supreme court to invalidate the Elks' contract, which the court did. The circumstances were more complex than portrayed in the narrative.
6. Graves to Olmsted Brothers, March 8, 1910; Olmsted Brothers to Smith, April 5, 1910 (LC). *Chr* Nov. 24, 1909, reports that Graves bought the 700-acre Dart farm for $16,000 to preserve the springs that supplied water for Waikiki.
7. For a discussion of the parks, see the author's "A. L. White, Champion of Urban Beauty."
8. White to Dawson, July 18, 1910 (LC); *SR* June 3, 1911; Spokane County mortgages 214:521 (Sept. 1, 1911). The house cost $20,000 to construct.
9. Elevations and floor plan are in the Cutter collection, EWSHS, L84-207.158 and L84-207.170. The description is based in part on the nomination for inclusion in the National Register of Historic Places, 1984.
10. Dawson notes, Dec. 3, 1910; Graves to Olmsted Brothers, March 8, 1910; Olmsted Brothers to Smith, April 5, 1910; Smith to Dawson, Jan. 8, 1912 (LC); *Chr* Dec. 13, 1912.
11. Estimates and bids are in the Cutter collection, EWSHS; Dawson notes, Dec. 3, 1910 (LC).
12. *SR* March 16, 1911 (Shaw and Borden); Dawson to Miss Bullard, Olmsted Brothers, Dec. 22, 1910 (emphasis his), to Smith, Dec. 5, 1911; Olmsted Brothers to Graves, Feb. 6, 1912 (LC).

13. Graves to Olmsted Brothers, June 18, 1936 (LC).

14. Graves's holdings are approximate because he added and sold property, gave some for road and power-line easements, etc. The estimate of 3,000 acres is from Spokane Presbytery minutes May 29, 1913, quoting Country Homes Co. Spokane County articles 366594, amended Feb. 17, 1913, with officers' names, 384981. Capitalized for $300,000. Stockholders paid in their stock with contributions of land. No market for stock was attempted.

15. See Gray, *Not by Might,* 87–89; Spokane Presbytery minutes, May 29, 1913, which contain the letter of May 23 quoted; Presbyterian Synod of Washington, 24th session (1913), minutes, 540; Board of Trustees, Whitworth, Sept. 26, 1913. Saylor's school was first called Lyon, then Saylor's, and then Spokane Academy, according to his advertisement, Dir 1918, p. 15. Saylor obituary, *SR* March 22, 1935.

16. *Chr* May 30, 1913; Spokane Presbytery minutes, May 29, 1913, gives financial status; Synod minutes (1913), 540, quotation; Brosnan, "Whitworth Story," 3–5.

17. Synod minutes (1913), 540; *Chr* May 30, 1913; Gray, *Not by Might,* 91, quotes Graves on $152,000 value of College Homes addition. An article in *Chr* March 9, 1912, says Graves paid $92,000 for 640 acres, suggesting a lower value for the college ground.

18. "Report of the trustees of Whitworth College," in Synod Minutes, 25th session (1914), 65–67, listing 14 Spokane men among 23 trustees; Gray, *Not by Might,* 88, suggests that Spokane's goal was $70,000 and the Synod would contribute $30,000; *SR* Oct. 17, 1913; April 5 and 29, 1914; *Chr* April 13, Aug. 3, 1913; April 12 and 27, 1914.

19. Spokane County deeds, 438268, in 329:334, Dec. 10, 1914; Spokane Presbytery minutes, May 29, 1913, and Oct. 1, 1914 (resolution quoted). The Presbytery would also have had the deed prohibit pool halls and games of chance, but Graves did not mention these in the deed.

20. Gray, *Not by Might,* 139, 169–70; *Whitworth College Bulletin,* 18:1 (May 1948), 1; *SR* Aug. 28, 1921 (house), Oct. 29, 1939.

21. Spokane County platbooks, S:16; Dir 1910; according to the Spokane *Press,* Nov. 23, 1909, the country club bought 250 acres from Graves at $250 an acre; see also Spokane County deeds 329:281 (Nov. 30, 1919). The firm of Neely and Walker, real estate, originally handled College Homes and other Graves property but in February 1915 Graves took over sales with his own company, Country Homes Development (with son Clyde and A. L. White). The caddy was John Sisk, later a noted professor at Gonzaga University and author of national repute.

22. Graves v. F. G. Dunlap, Spokane County civil 43585 (1914); Washington State supreme court 12510 (1915). Graves was fined $50 by the county.

23. Milan Farms, Spokane County articles 401538, Aug. 29, 1913; list of officers 409736. The Washington Mill Co. men were J. C. Barline and Judson W. Cook: *SR* Nov. 30, 1913, sec. 4, Milan; May 13–17, 1915, dogs. Milan Farms lands are scattered tracts rather than a block of acreage, in T29, T20, and T31N, R43, R44, and R45 EWM, in Spokane and Pend Oreille counties. They are pictured on a poster, 1925, in the Shaw and Borden collection, EWSHS. Graves employed Clarence H. Stewart, an engineer from St. Paul, to lay out and install an irrigation system that would draw water from Sacheen Lake for Milan Farms. Stewart previously had served as chief of construction for the Spokane & Inland Empire and as chief of a locating party for the proposed extension into the Big Bend. He would be best known as resident engineer, later on, for the Hibbing Power Plant in Minnesota. File 17 in the Stewart papers, Minnesota Historical Society, contains approximately three dozen sheets of reports, estimates, tables of water use, and similar documents relating to Stewart's service with Graves. Edward Nolan, archivist, EWSHS, called Stewart's papers to my attention.

24. White to Olmsted Brothers, Feb. 6 and May 26, 1915; Oct. 5 and 10, 1916; Aug. 30 and Sept. 13, 1920 (LC); Spokane County mortgages 334:314, providing that all monies fall due if payments are in default, and release three months after due date; interviews with Janice Howe, Graves's great-granddaughter, and Louise ("Burr") Willis, White's daughter.

25. Book map of Country Homes Estates, auction by C. A. Austin and Co., auctioneers (EWSHS); sales based on Spokane County deeds grantor index 1913–28. Brochure, Shaw and Bowden collection, EWSHS, quotation.

26. *Chr* July 4, 1912, June 20, 1915, golf; *SR* Sept. 23, 1918; Mrs. Clyde Graves, *SR* Dec. 17, 1918; Howe interview, "adventuress"; Alice obit., *SR* Aug. 15, 1959. According to *Chr* July 28, 1928, Alice inherited several houses and lots in Illinois and $54,171 from her mother's estate.

27. Howe interview; transcript of Nancy G. Compau's interview with Ward Bronson, Graves's chauffeur 1924–31; the Davenports' register for 1921 (EWSHS). In a personal sketch for a newspaper, Graves mentions that he is president of the Whitworth Community Church.

28. *SR* Oct. 9, 1921, Feb. 15, 1922; Exchange Bank papers (WSU, container 22) show Nicholls's circumstances on Nov. 15, 1922. According to *Chr* Aug. 7, 1924, Graves paid the money for $121,000 in Granby stock

which he did not receive. EWSHS holds 43 8×10-inch negatives of photographic copies of investment accounts for Jay, Clyde, and Amanda Graves, 1911–21, evidently shot for exhibits in a lawsuit. The broker is not identified. They show active trading in Granby and modest investments by Jay Graves in Anaconda, Kennecott, Butte and Superior, and other mining stocks.

29. *Mining Truth,* 11:14 (Sept. 1, 1926), 37–38; Bronson interview.

30. *Mining Truth,* 13:14 (Sept. 1, 1928), 25; *Mining Congress Journal,* 15:9 (Sept. 1929), 667–68; *Wallace Miner,* Jan. 21, 1917; March 27, 1930; Aug. 3, 1933. This last *Miner* names William R. Fisher, Long Beach, Calif., as financier of Constitution. See Edward L. Jones, "Reconnaissance of Pine Creek," 15–16. Rutter to G. L. Fairbank, Nov. 1, 1930 (Howe). The Constitution eventually was sold to the Spokane-Idaho Co., a closed corporation.

31. Spokane County mortgages 360:595 and T:347. Graves consolidated his encumbered ground in 1925 in the Waikiki Farms Co., with capital of $500 and stock of no stated value, later amended to increase capital stock to $50,000. There were three directors, each of whom held one share, Graves and two employees. Waikiki Farms, Spokane County articles of incorporation 813706, Aug. 20, 1925, amended by 825854, Nov. 25, 1925. Bronson interview.

32. Bronson interview; Ann Blake Graves letter to Howe, Feb. 22, 1987, answering author's questions; Spokane County civil 79980, State v. Milan Farms, July 15, 1927. Kimmel was employed by the Old National and Union Trust Co. 1911–58. *SR* Oct. 16, 1968, Kimmel obituary. The two suits against Milan Farms properties, both dated 1918, involved Century Life Assurance and Pacific Northwest Investment companies.

33. Mortgage release for 417 acres, Feb. 26, 1937, Spokane County mortgages 458:469; sale to Marr, *Chr* Jan. 6, 1937; Spokane County deeds 472:42 (Marr paid in part by deeding his home at W. 204 Sixteenth to Waikiki Farms). Graves's address, 1821 Upper Terrace, sold to W. W. Witherspoon. Marr's heirs sold Waikiki for $86,400 in 1963 (deed 984732B, Dec. 19, 1963) to a syndicate of seven, which sold it on July 1, 1983, to Gonzaga University for $400,000.

34. Howe interview and letter (Howe).

35. Frank Graves, *SR* Jan. 20, 1948; Jay Graves, Probate Pasadena P-8062, Los Angeles County Superior Court.

36. Warren to Alice Graves, May 3, 1948; Bean to Alice Graves, undated (Howe).

Bibliography

The following list of sources does not contain legal reports, selected city and county documents, legislative acts, deed and plat books, annual reports, or similar items cited in full in the notes.

Apparently, no body of Graves business documents exists. The Granby files, acquired by Consolidated Mining and Smelting (Cominco) when Granby sold its assets at Anyox, B.C., in July 1935, apparently were destroyed in a "housecleaning" of outdated records. C. George Miller, managing director of the Mining Association of Canada, Ottawa, furnished a 1910 annual report of Granby that contains a historical summary, comparative data on dividends and production, and the Sussman report that caused a stockholders uproar in 1910.

ARCHIVAL SOURCES

The Minnesota Historical Society, in its manuscripts and archives division, St. Paul, holds extensive documents on the Spokane & Inland Empire Railway and its subsidiaries. The Society provides comprehensive finding aids. I relied primarily on presidents' correspondence files of the Great Northern and Northern Pacific, S&IE minutes, and statements of accounts of Northern Pacific branch lines, subsidiaries, and related companies, and on histories and corporate records of Great Northern subsidiaries. Annual reports of the NP and GN, held by Minnesota, are available on microfilm.

The James Jerome Hill Reference Library, St. Paul, houses the papers of James and Louis W. Hill, arranged and indexed by Grace Lee Nute. The papers consist of correspondence, reports, scrapbooks of clippings, and ephemera, representing thirty-five distinct businesses. There are categories for individuals, subjects, and geographic areas. Some letterbooks have been filmed for use in the Library.

The Massachusetts Historical Society, Boston, holds approximately eighty linear feet of unprocessed "office" papers of the Adams family and Real Estate Trust. These were brought to my attention by Peter Drummey, associate librarian, and searched by Katherine H. Griffin, cataloguer of manuscripts. They are essential to understanding the Adams investments in Spokane real estate. The processed and indexed collection of Adams documents does not contain references to Spokane.

The Provincial Archives of British Columbia, Victoria, hold the Cominco papers, 1884–1965 (MSS 15), with some Granby correspondence in volume 2/1, a microfilmed contract between Graves and Granby (reel B4417, file 256/1897), and a wealth of published and unpublished data relating to mining and provincial affairs, with useful finding aids. The archives have, as well, an impressive collection of newspapers of British Columbia, many on film, for use in the reference room. A list of newspapers is available.

Letters of Thomas G. Shaughnessy, during his service with the Canadian Pacific, are contained in numbered letterbooks (MG 28, III 20) in the Public Archives of Canada, Ottawa. Some letters up to December 31, 1901, also remain in the files of CP Rail, Montreal, and were furnished by Dave Jones, assistant archivist. The letterbooks have been microfilmed. The Public Archives also hold numerous documents relating to railway and canal authorizations and construction. For data used in this study, I relied on the register and journals, 1879–1906, of railways and canals, Railway Branch (RG43, A II, vol. 126: subject 726, Columbia & Western; subject 740, Vancouver, Victoria & Eastern).

The bulk of correspondence of Olmsted Brothers resides in the manuscripts division of the Library of Congress, Washington, D.C., and may be examined on sixty microfilm reels. Series B, the firm's job files 1871–1950, consists of correspondence and memoranda filed by client name and a number assigned by Olmsted Brothers. Finding aids include reel 1, an alphabetical index to the collection, and reel 7, a geographic index by name of city, client, and job number. For this study, I selected only those clients listed under Spokane who seemed to be associated with Graves in some manner.

Papers of the Crow's Nest Pass Coal Company, Ltd., 1888–1975 (M 1561) are contained in seventy-five document boxes in the archives of the Glenbow-Alberta Institute, Calgary. The papers include correspondence, reports, printed materials, and clipping files. There is an excellent container list.

The International Union of Mine, Mill and Smelter Workers (Canada) collection includes papers of the Western Federation of Miners. It is housed in the archives at the University of British Columbia, Vancouver. For this study, I used correspondence from boxes 147 and 157.

Spokane city and county records have been divided; those not in current use, with exceptions such as court and deed records, have been transferred to regional archives at Eastern Washington University, Cheney. The city and county retain deed, mortgage, legal, and other files both historical and current. Minutes of the city park board remain with the city. A user must rely largely on indexes prepared by city or county.

The Washington Water Power Company has current files on finance and operations and such historical documents as land titles, minutes, annual reports, and similar items. What noncurrent papers remain were divided between Washington State University, Pullman, which has the correspondence and many reports, and Eastern Washington University, with a lesser holding of mimeographed and printed materials. Washington State University has compiled a useful container guide.

Records of the Exchange National Bank (defunct), Spokane, are also in the Washington State University archives with a container guide. Certain records of other Spokane banks, both merged and dissolved, are in the files of the Comptroller, National Archives. The material in these bank records pertaining to Graves is revealing but sparse.

The Presbytery of the Inland Empire, Spokane, has two reels of microfilmed minutes of the Presbytery, formerly the Spokane Presbytery. Reel 1 (1890–1936) contains the material on Graves's gift of land to Whitworth College. Both the Presbyterian Synod of Alaska Northwest, Seattle, and Whitworth College have runs of Synod minutes, which were printed for general distribution among the presbyteries.

In addition to these various archives, I used selected items from the Northwestern and Pacific Hypotheekbank, the Kirtland K. Cutter, and the Shaw and Borden collections of the Eastern Washington State Historical Society. Anyone wishing to use these should consult the publication by Edward W. Nolan, *A Guide to the Manuscript Collections in the Eastern Washington State Historical Society* (Spokane, 1987). Certain documents relating to Granby were supplied by Tiny J. Gates, legal administrator, from the files of its successor, Zapata Corporation, Houston.

INTERVIEWS

Two interviews helped establish the general framework for this study of Graves: one, with the late Margaret Bean, on November 14, 1979, and the other, with the late Ford S. Barrett, on February 26, 1976. Miss Bean recalled her impressions of Graves, and Barrett commented on the physical growth of Spokane and on some of the developers. I also talked with the late Janice Graves Howe, J. P. Graves's great-granddaughter, who recalled her impressions of Graves, passed along family stories, allowed me to use letters, and wrote to Ann Blake Graves to ask some questions for me.

Nancy G. Compau, Spokane historian, interviewed Ward Bronson, Graves's chauffeur from 1924 to 1931, and allowed me to use her transcript. Bronson's recollections were largely personal.

UNPUBLISHED

"A Brief History and Description of the 'Phoenix' Operation." Typescript, Granby Mining Co., Ltd., 1971 (Zapata).

Church, John S. "Mining Companies in the West Kootenay and Boundary Regions of British Columbia, 1890–1900, Capital Formation and Financial Operations." Master's thesis, University of British Columbia, 1947.

Eastern Townships Bank, "Proceedings: 42nd Annual Meeting of Shareholders," June 5, 1901.

Green, Michael K. "Politics and Kilowatts: The Washington Water Power Company and Public Power, 1918–1941." Master's thesis, University of Idaho, 1962.

"History of Properties Comprising the Spokane & Inland Empire Railroad Company." 3 vols., typescript, May 1, 1919. Northern Pacific President's file 9128, Minnesota Historical Society. A receiver's report.

Howe, Janice Graves. "Graves Genealogy." Typescript, 1968, amended 1973.

McCulloch, A. "Railway Development in Southern British Columbia from 1890 on, and Some Reasons for Building the Kettle Valley Railway, and the Lines of the Vancouver, Victoria and Eastern Railway and Navigation Company in British Columbia." November 1938.

Mutschler, Charles V. "Street Railway Development in Spokane." Master's thesis, Eastern Washington University, 1981. Subsequently published.

Proxy Statement to Shareholders re: Proposed Amalgamation of Granby, Granisle, and Zapata Canada, Ltd., November 13, 1978 (Zapata).

Roy, Patricia E. "Railways, Politicians, and the Development of Vancouver as a Metropolitan Centre." Master's thesis, University of Toronto, 1963.

Strahorn, Robert E. "Ninety Years of Boyhood." Typescript memoirs, Strahorn Library, College of Idaho, Caldwell, 1942. Copies in other regional libraries.

Washington Water Power Co. "Statement A: Outline of Origin and Development." Statement to the Federal Power Commission, May 1937.

BOOKS

Athearn, Robert G. *Union Pacific Country*. Chicago: Rand McNally, 1971.
Barman, Jean. *West beyond the West: A History of British Columbia*. Toronto: University of Toronto Press, 1991.
Benedict, C. Harry. *Red Metal: The Calumet and Hecla Story*. Ann Arbor: University of Michigan Press, 1952.
Berton, Pierre. *The Impossible Railway*. New York: Alfred A. Knopf, 1972.
Canada 1893. N.p., 1893. Gazeteer and business handbook.
Cavin, Ruth. *Trolleys: Riding and Remembering the Electric Interurban Railways*. New York: Hawthorne Books, 1976.
Decker, Donald M., and Mary L. Decker. *Reflections on Elegance: Pasadena's Huntington Hotel since 1906*. Laguna Niguel: Royal Literary Publishers, 1984.
den Otter, A. A. *Civilizing the West: The Galts and the Development of Western Canada*. Edmonton: University of Alberta Press, 1982.
Durham, Nelson W. *History of the City of Spokane and Spokane Country, Washington, from Its Earliest Settlement to the Present Time*. 3 vols. Spokane: S. J. Clarke Publishing Co., 1912.
Dyar, Ralph E. *News for an Empire: The Story of the "Spokesman-Review" of Spokane, Washington, and of the Field It Serves*. Caldwell, Idaho: Caxton Printers, 1952.
Eagle, John A. *The Canadian Pacific Railroad and Development of Western Canada, 1896–1914*. Kingston, Ont.: McGill-Queen's University, 1989.
Fahey, John. *The Ballyhoo Bonanza: Charles Sweeny and the Idaho Mines*. Seattle: University of Washington Press, 1971.
———. *Inland Empire: D. C. Corbin and Spokane*. Seattle: University of Washington Press, 1965.
Gray, Alfred O. *Not by Might: The Story of Whitworth College, 1890–1965*. Spokane: Whitworth College, 1965.
Gregg, T. *A History of Hancock County, Illinois*. N.p., 1968.
Herfindahl, Orris C. *Copper Costs and Prices: 1870–1957*. Baltimore: Johns Hopkins Press, 1959.
Hidy, Ralph W., Muriel E. Hidy, and Roy V. Scott, with Don L. Hofsommer. *The Great Northern Railway: A History*. Boston: Harvard Business School Press, 1988.
Hilton, George W., and John F. Due. *Electric Interurban Railways in America*. Rev. ed. Stanford: Stanford University Press, 1964.
Howay, F. W., W. N. Sage, and H. F. Angus. *British Columbia and the United States*. Toronto: Ryerson Press, 1942.

Innis, Harold A. *A History of the Canadian Pacific Railway*. Toronto: University of Toronto Press, 1971.
Kennedy, W. G. *History of the Rossland Subdivision*. Calgary: Calgary Group of British Railway Remodellers of North America, 1983. For railroad buffs.
Lee, Everett S., Ann Ratner Miller, Carol P. Brainerd, and Richard A. Easterlin. *Population Redistribution and Economic Growth of the United States, 1870–1950*. 2 vols. Philadelphia: American Philosophical Society, 1957.
LeRoy, Osmond E. *The Geology and Ore Deposits of Phoenix, Boundary District, British Columbia*. Department of Mines, Geological Survey Branch, Memoir 21. Ottawa: Government Printing Bureau, 1912.
Morgan, Henry James, ed. *Canadian Men and Women of the Time: A Handbook of Canadian Biography of Living Characters*. 2d ed. Toronto: William Briggs, 1912.
Mutschler, Charles V., with Clyde L. Parent and Wilmer H. Siegert. *Spokane's Street Railways: An Illustrated History*. Spokane: Inland Empire Railway History Society, 1987.
Nagel, Paul C. *Descent from Glory: Four Generations of the John Adams Family*. New York: Oxford University Press, 1983.
Newspaper Reference Book of Canada. Toronto: Press Publishing, 1903.
Ramsey, Bruce. *Ghost Towns of British Columbia*. Vancouver: Mitchell Press, 1963.
Reavis, John R. *City of Spokane*. Spokane: Clough and Graves, 1891.
Rudin, Ronald. *Banking en Français: The French Banks of Québec*. Toronto: University of Toronto Press, 1985.
Sanford, Barrie. *McCulloch's Wonder: Story of the Kettle Valley Railway*. 3d ed. North Vancouver: Whitecap Books, 1981.
Schwantes, Carlos A. *Radical Heritage: Labor, Socialism, and Reform in Washington and British Columbia*. Seattle: University of Washington Press, 1979.
Smith, Adam. *Wealth of Nations*. New York: Modern Library, 1937.
Soden, Dale E. *A Venture of Mind and Spirit: An Illustrated History of Whitworth College*. Spokane: Whitworth College, 1990.
Spokane Blue Book, 1902–03. Spokane: Stage Publishing, 1902.
Spokane City Plan Commission, *Needs and Resources for Improving Spokane*, Vol. 1: *Community Renewal Study*. Spokane: City Plan Commission, September 1965.
Spokane Park Commission. *Report of the Board of Park Commissioners, 1891–1913*. Spokane: Board of Park Commissioners, 1913.

Taylor, G. W. *Mining: The History of Mining in British Columbia.* Saanichton, B.C.: Hancock House Publishers, 1978.

Turner, Robert D. *Sternwheelers and Steam Tugs: An Illustrated History of the Canadian Pacific Railway's British Columbia Lake and River Service.* Victoria: Sono Nis Press, 1984.

———. *West of the Great Divide: An Illustrated History of the Canadian Pacific Railway in British Columbia, 1880–1986.* Victoria: Sono Nis Press, 1987.

U.S. Federal Trade Commission. *Report on the Copper Industry.* Washington: Government Printing Office, 1947.

Warner, Sam Bass, Jr. *Streetcar Suburbs: The Process of Growth in Boston, 1790–1900.* Cambridge: Harvard University Press, 1962.

ARTICLES AND PAMPHLETS

Baillie, A. S. "A Half-Century of Mining in British Columbia: The Granby Story." *Western Miner* 22:7 (July 1949): reprint.

Bean, Margaret. "Waikiki Beauty Spot on Little Spokane." *Spokesman-Review*, Feb. 24, 1957.

"Book Map of Country Homes Estates." Spokane: Charles S. Austin Co., Auctioneers, October 1921.

"Boundary Creek District: The Town of Grand Forks and the Granby Smelter." *[B.C.] Mining Record* 7:6 (June 1900): 207–13.

Brock, R. W. "Ore Deposits of the Boundary (Creek) District, B.C." *Journal of the Canadian Mining Institute* 5 (1902): 365–78.

Brosnan, C. J. "Whitworth Story." *Spokesman-Review* magazine, Jan. 3, 1954.

Campbell, C. M. "The Granby Mines and Phoenix," Canadian Mining Institute *Transactions* 22 (1919): 155–79.

———. "Granby Mining Methods." *Journal of the Canadian Mining Institute* 11 (1908): 392–406.

Carmichael, Herbert. "Mineral Locations: Portland Canal District." British Columbia Bureau of Mines, *Bulletin 1* (1909).

"Electric Railway Developments." *Scientific American Supplement No. 1606* (Oct. 13, 1906): 25738–39.

"Electric Railways in and about Spokane." *Electric Railway Journal* 34:14 (Oct. 2, 1909): 524–28.

Fahey, John. "A. L. White, Champion of Urban Beauty." *Pacific Northwest Quarterly* 72:4 (Oct. 1981): 170–79.

———. "Longest Crap Game in the West." *Spokane* 4:3 (March 1980): 37, 54–56. On the Spokane Stock Exchange.

———. "Power Plays: The Enigma of Little Falls." *Pacific Northwest Quarterly* 82:4 (October 1991): 122–31.

———. "When the Dutch Owned Spokane." *Pacific Northwest Quarterly* 72:1 (January 1981): 2–10.

Friedricks, William. "Henry E. Huntington and Real Estate Development in Southern California, 1898–1917." *Southern California Quarterly* 71 (4): 327–41.

"Granby: 1899 to 1974 and Beyond." *Western Miner* (June 1974): reprint.

Hanbury-Williams, Charles. "In the Kootenays." *Blackwood's* (April 1903): 494–507.

Harkin, W. A. "A. C. Flumerfelt." *Westward Ho! Magazine* 2 (February 1908): 15–18.

Hodges, A. B. W. "Handling Three Thousand Tons of Ore per Day at the Granby Mines and Smelter, Phoenix and Grand Forks, B.C.," Canadian Mining Institute *Transactions* 11 (1908): 407–14.

Hook, Harry H., and Francis J. McGuire. *Spokane Falls Illustrated . . . Portraits and Sketches of Leading Citizens.* Minneapolis: Frank L. Thresher, 1889.

[Hulteng, John.] *Meeting Place by the Lake: An Informal History of Hayden Lake Golf and Country Club.* Spokane: Hayden Lake Golf and Country Club, 1986.

"Hydro-Electric Power Plant of the Inland Empire System." *Electric Railway Journal* 32:19 (Oct. 10, 1909): 898–902.

"Inland Empire Faced Hard Problems." *Electric Railway Journal* 51:17 (April 27, 1918): 825.

Jennings, Frederick. "The Most Notable Architecture and Landscape Architecture of Spokane, Washington." *Architect and Engineer* 65:3 (June 1921): 46–94.

Jones, Edward L., Jr. "Reconnaissance of the Pine Creek District, Idaho." United States Geological Service *Bulletin 710-A*. Washington: Government Printing Office, 1919.

Kalez, Jay J. "Liberty Lake: Boom, Bust, Boom." *Spokane Daily Chronicle*, June 25, 1966.

Keffer, Frederic. "Notes on Mining and Smelting in the Boundary District, B.C." *Journal of the Canadian Mining Institute* 7 (1904): 142–46.

Keller, Glenda, and Alice M. Evans. "Brief History of Railways in the Boundary Area." Boundary Historical Society *10th Annual Report* (1985): 46–65.

Kirker, G. B., and L. S. Haskins. "The Spokane & Inland Empire Railroad." *Electric Journal* 8:10 (Oct. 1911): 858–69.

Ledoux, Albert A. "Production of Copper in the Boundary District, B.C." *Journal of the Canadian Mining Institute* 5 (1902): 171–77.

"Manito Park—from Teepee to Mansion." Spokane: Spokane-Washington Improvement Co., 1909.

"Manito Park Homesites: Price List, February 1909." Spokane: Spokane-Washington Improvement Co., 1909.

Morse, Lewis Kennedy. "The Price-Fixing of Copper." *Quarterly Journal of Economics* 33 (November 1918): 71–106.

Nagel, Paul C. "A West That Failed: The Dream of Charles Francis Adams II." *Western Historical Quarterly* 18:4 (October 1987): 397–407.

Nolan, Edward W. *A Guide to the Cutter Collection.* Spokane: Eastern Washington State Historical Society, 1984.

Olmsted, Frederick L., Jr. "The Town-Planning Movement in America." *Annals of the American Academy of Political and Social Science* 51 (January 1914): 179.

"Packhorse Smote Granby Rock with Hoof and Caused Millions to Flow Forth." *Spokesman-Review*, Sept. 14, 1913.

"Passenger Stations on the Inland Empire System." *Electric Railway Journal* 32:24 (Nov. 14, 1908): 1372.

Peterson, Jon A. "City Beautiful Movement: Forgotten Origins and Lost Meanings." *Journal of Urban History* 2 (1976): 419–27.

"Prosperous Trolleys." *Review of Reviews* 39:5 (May 1909): 634.

Roy, Patricia E. "Progress, Prosperity, and Politics: The Railway Policies of Richard McBride." *BC Studies* 47 (Autumn 1980): 3–28.

Rudin, Ronald. "Naissance et déclin d'une élite locale: la Banque des Cantons de l'Est, 1859–1912." *Revue d'histoire de l'amérique française (1947)* 38:2 (Autumn 1984): 165–79.

Sherbrooke Commercial and Industrial Edition. N.p., n.d. From files of the Montreal Public Library.

Siegert, Wilmer H. "This and That from the Twenties: Our Electric Interurban Trains Were Fast and on Time." *Pacific Northwesterner* 26:1 (Winter 1982): 1–5.

Spokane Water Department *First Annual Report* (1911). Spokane: City Water Department, 1911.

Stark, Lawrence R. "Lewiston-Clarkston Improvement Company: City Planner in Southeastern Washington." *Record 1975*, Friends of the Library, Washington State University, 36 (1975): 59–70.

Strachan, Robert. "Coal Mining Industry of Western Canada." Second (Triennial) Empire Mining and Metallurgy Congress *Proceedings* (Edmonton, Alta., 1928), pt. 2:1–90.

"Traffic Features." *Electric Railway Journal* 36:15 (Oct. 8, 1910): 630–42.

Van Deusen, Edgar, "Electric Interurban Railway Bonds as Investments." *Annals of the American Society of Political and Social Science* 30:2 (September 1907): 144–57.

White, Aubrey Lee. "Granby Mine Developed from a Shoestring." *Spokesman-Review* magazine, Jan. 15, 1928.

———. "Granby Named for French-Canadian Village." *Spokesman-Review* magazine, Jan. 22, 1928.

———. "Granby Ore Body Eclipsed Greatest Known." *Spokesman-Review* magazine, Jan. 29, 1928.

———. "Granby Shareholders Netted Excellent Profit." *Spokesman-Review* magazine, Feb. 5, 1928.

———. "Granby Escaped Serious Labor Troubles." *Spokesman-Review* magazine, Feb. 12, 1928.

———. "Granby Tonnage Brought Railway Conflict." *Spokesman-Review* magazine, Feb. 19, 1928.

———. "Granby Turns Attention to Hidden Creek." *Spokesman-Review* magazine, Feb. 26, 1928.

———. "Granby Produced 11,000,000 Tons of Copper." *Spokesman-Review* magazine, March 4, 1928.

———. "Granby's Anyox Smelter Is Empire's Largest." *Spokesman-Review* magazine, March 11, 1928.

White, William P. "New Plant and Equipment at the Constitution Mine." *Mining Congress Journal* 15:9 (September 1929): 667–68.

Wilcox, W. B. "Early History of Granby." *Northwest Mining Truth* 51 (Feb. 16, 1920): 19–20.

Index

Adams, Brooks: buys Spokane land, 32; pushes brother aside, 40; supports terminal rates, 48
Adams, Charles Francis II: buys Spokane land, 32; western investments, 40; supports military post, 47–48; Cannon Hill development, 48, 114n30; sells Lincoln Heights, 50, 114n34
Adams, George C., 32, 40
Adams Real Estate Trust: buys in Spokane, 32; Spokane holdings, 40–41, 112n12 and n13
Aldridge, Walter, 16, 75; manages Trail smelter, 12; and freight rates, 13; opposes second smelter, 20
Anyox. *See* Hidden Creek
Automobiles, 70–71

Baker, George F., Jr., 60, 63, 79, 80
Bean, Margaret: writes on Graves, 100–102
Blackwell, Frederick A.: description, 54, 115n1; builds Coeur d'Alene & Spokane Railroad, 54–55; and Coeur d'Alene parkland, 60, 117n14; acquires Spokane & Inland Empire stock, 61; plans new railroad, 41, 61–62
Boundary mines, British Columbia: early development, 6–7; political importance, 8; routes to, 9; growth, 14; reports on, 16–17
British Columbia Copper Company, Ltd., 6, 81, 83
Brown, David: and Rockwood addition, 47–48, 52, 53

Canadian Mining Review: criticizes Granby capitalization, 18
Canadian Pacific Railway: trackage in British Columbia, 9; builds to Midway, B.C., 10; Trail freight rates, 13; Phoenix traffic, 17; subsidizes Spokane International Railroad, 80; and Crow's Nest Pass agreement, 105n15. *See also* Shaughnessy, Thomas G.
Cannon Hill district, Spokane. *See* Adams, Charles Francis II
City Beautiful movement, 33
Clark, F. Lewis: president of exposition, 26; business interests, 30–31, 32, 40, 41, 110n22; and S&IE, 55, 61, 67
Clark, George C., 79
Clough, Charles F.: Graves's partner, 24, 26–27, 28, 30, 108n4; breaks with Graves, 31
Coeur d'Alene & Spokane Railroad: construction, 30, 54–55, 115n1; terminal, 41
Coeur d'Alene Lake, 67
Colfax Commoner: on Graves's railroad, 57
Columbia & Western Railway: Canadian Pacific acquires, 9; history, 105n14
Constitution mine, Idaho, 99, 100
Cook, Francis H.: 29, 109n19, 111n1; loses Montrose line, 35
Coolidge, Alfred: in electric railroad company, 55; in real estate company, 57
Copper: price rigging, 16; demand of 1904–7, 81; falling prices, 82

INDEX

Copper Mountain mines, B.C., 87
Corbaley, Gordon C., 51
Corbin, Daniel C., 32, 58, 68; proposes British Columbia railroad, 9; builds Spokane International Railroad, 79–80
Country Homes Development Company: organized, 92–93; gives land for Whitworth College, 94–95; land sales, 97, 125n21
Cowles, William H., 32, 40, 94; as publisher, 33, 97; in Cannon Hill development, 48; in paper mill company, 65; and parklands, 90
Cox, George S.: president of Crow's Nest Pass Coal Company, 75, 82
Crow's Nest Pass, Canada: railroad to, 16
Crow's Nest Pass Coal Company: organized, 75; performance, 75–76, 82; Hill buys control, 82, 123n21
Cutter, Kirtland K., 89, 90, 91

Davenport, Louis M., 90
Davidson, W. C., 61
Dawson, J. Frederick: confers on Spokane designs, 39–40; park plan, 90; on Graves's payments, 92
Depressions: in 1893, 29, 32–33; in 1907, 65–66
Dominion Copper Company, B.C., 14
Duncan, John W., 48
Dyer, E. J., 76

Eastern Townships Bank, Canada, 8; branches in Boundary, 14, 107n34; loan to Granby, 18; Graves's indebtedness, 19; loan to S&IE, 66
Elliott, Howard, 44, 52; tries to thwart Graves, 55, 60; on Graves's electric railroad, 60; complains of traffic, 67; resists Graves's extension plans, 70; on Graves's Spokane reputation, 71
Engineering & Mining Journal: on report of Granby bottoming, 84, 85
Ethics: in business, 25

Exchange National Bank of Spokane, 19, 76

Ferris, Esta Maud (Mrs. Frank Graves), 23
Ferris, Joel E., 90
Finch, John A., 29, 32, 90; develops Audubon, 43–44; in Cannon Hill development, 48
First Trust and Savings, Chicago, 61, 63
Flumerfelt, Alfred C.: S. H. C. Miner's spy, 18; president of International Coal and Coke Company, 15, 74, 76

Galer, H. N., 15, 76
Gault, Charles E., 82; stockholder in Graves's companies, 11; drops out, 18
Glasgow, Samuel, 49
Granby, Quebec, 7
Granby Consolidated Mining and Smelting Company, Ltd.: organized, 10–11, 106n21; stock sales, 13; builds smelter, 13–14; and miners' union, 14, 83; matte sales, 17; reorganized in 1901, 17–18; in *Canadian Mining Review*, 18; custom ores, 19; buys Kettle Falls power site, 65; expands mineral claims, 75; directors of, 77, 79; production 1903–5, 80–81; converts capital stock, 81; place in industry, 82; and ore shortages, 82, 83; 1910 report of scandal, 84–85; record production of 1912, 86; last Phoenix ore, 86; closes Grand Forks smelter, 87. *See also* Hidden Creek
Granby smelter, 4. *See also* Granby Consolidated Mining and Smelting Company, Ltd.
Grand Forks, B.C.: smelter at, 6, 87
Graves, Amanda (Mrs. J. P. Graves), 4, 5, 98; contributes to Waikiki, 92
Graves, Blanche Flournoy (Mrs. Clyde Graves), 88, 98
Graves, Clyde, 23, 92, 93; carline

INDEX 141

as business, 35; manages S&IE, 63, 67, 71; marriage and children, 88; manages Milan Farms, 96; remarriage, 98; death, 101
Graves, Frank, 22–23, 32, 38, 43, 96, 101, 110n23
Graves, Jay Paul: description, 3; acquires Boundary mines, 5–6; meets S. H. C. Miner, 7; and Granby, 10–11, 16, 18–19, 20–21, 74–87 passim; and matte sales, 17; early years and family, 22–24; in real estate, 24–27, 38–39, 57; as mayoral candidate, 28; relations with F. Lewis Clark, 30–31; bids on city water warrants, 31, 110n24; acquires Montrose railroad, 35; and Spokane Traction Company, 35–36, 41, 51; organizes Spokane-Washington Improvement Company, 37–38; develops Manito district, 38–39; owns baseball team, 42; rivalry with Washington Water Power, 42–44, 52; offers to buy lines, 43; opens residential areas, 44; develops Rockwood extension, 47–48, 53; in Coeur d'Alene & Spokane Railroad Co., 54–55; plans electric railroad, 55, 116n4; organizes Spokane & Inland Railway, 55–60; hires advertising man, 60; needs railroad money, 61, 66; and S&IE stock, 61; and preferred "rights," 62, 118n20; and James J. Hill, 62, 65; develops Nine Mile powersite, 63–64, 65, 119n23; on earnings, 66; and S&IE, 66, 68–71; relations with Crow's Nest Pass Coal Company, 75, 82; visits Hidden Creek site, 83–84; chateau plans, 88; farm, 88–89, 96; and Spokane Club, 89; plans Waikiki, 89–90, 91; country land development, 92, 97; and Whitworth College, 94–95; falls out with White, 97; finances and investments, 97–98, 100, 127n31; loses Waikiki, Country Homes, 99–100; death, 101–2; and state college location, 109n11
Graves, Mary Alice (second Mrs. J. P. Graves), 98, 100, 101
Graves, Will, 50, 76; on value of Graves's stocks, 51–52; in electric railroad company, 55; and S&IE stock, 61, 62
Graves family: in Illinois, 23, 108n3 and n4
Gray, Carl R., 71
Great Northern Railway: acquires Spokane Falls & Northern Railroad, 10, 106n17; builds to Boundary, 15–16; Phoenix line, 77; Boundary freight, 80. *See also* Hill, James Jerome
Greenwood, B.C., 9–10
Grinnell, Fred B., 44, 53; sells Manito area, 38–39, 47; in railroad real estate company, 57; joins S&IE board, 67

Ham, David T., 58, 60
Hayden Lake Improvement Company, 60
Held, Albert, 60, 117n13
Hemenway, John F., 6
Hensel, Gustav A., 56
Hereshoff, J. B. F., 74
Hidden Creek mines: and Granby, 83–84, 85, 86; development of, 85–86
Higginson, Henry Lee, 55, 79
Hill, James Jerome: 3, 52, 79; and British Columbia railroads, 10; buys Victoria, Vancouver & Eastern charter, 15; builds to Boundary, 15–16; joins scheme to buy Granby, 20; and S&IE, 62, 69, 118n22; gives Graves unusable check, 65; and Crow's Nest Coal Company, 75, 76, 121n7; enters British Columbia, 76–77; visits Phoenix, 80; urged to buy Granby, 86; death, 87. *See also* Spokane Falls & Northern Railroad

INDEX

Hill, Louis: denies promises to Graves, 54, 115n2; fires Graves, 71
Hillyard, Wash., 41
Hodges, Abel B. W.: manages Granby smelter, 11–12; named general manager of Granby Con, 77; on labor relations, 83; resigns, 84
Hogan, Frank P., 32, 40, 46; donates parkland, 38; develops Summit area, 41; develops Audubon, 43–44; sells Bowl and Pitcher, 65
Houghton, Clement S., 74
Hutton, Levi W., 42

Improvement clubs, Spokane, 42
Inland Empire Railway, 61, 73. *See also* Spokane & Inland Empire Railroad
International Coal and Coke Company, 76
Interurban railways: as investments, 56, 116n7; in Pacific Northwest, 56; town reactions to, 57

James, Arthur C., 79
Jones, Arthur D., 40, 41; and Cannon Hill development, 44, 48–49; in Graves's company, 57; and Liberty Lake lands, 60

Kiernan, William H., 50–51
Knob Hill mine, B.C., 4, 6, 10
Kuhn, Aaron, 61

Lake Superior Company, Mich., 62
Langeloth, Jacob: Granby director, 74; president of Granby, 77, 79, 82
Lawyer, Jay, 50–51
Ledoux, Albert: Boundary mines report, 16–17; on second smelter, 20
Ledoux and Company, New York, 16
LeRoi mine, B.C., 5, 9
Liberty Lake, Wash., 60, 67
Liftchild, Charles, 43, 46
Lincoln Heights district, Spokane, 50–51, 53, 114n34
Lindsey, G. G. S., 75

Linsley, "Colonel" Nelson E.: inspects Old Ironsides mine, 8; inspects coal claims, 76
Luther, George M., 74, 79

Malloy, John S., 49
Malloy, William C., 49
Manito Park, Spokane, 38, 111n7
Marr, Charles E., 101
Mellen, Charles S., 54, 115n3
Milan Farms, 96, 97, 126n23
Miner, Stephen H. C.: meets Graves, 7; organizes Granby, 10–11, 16; ousted as Granby Con president, 74, 79
Mining Truth: editorial on S&IE stocks, 70
Montrose street railway, Spokane, 35, 54, 111n1

Nicholls, Walter A., 98, 99
Nichols, William H.: buys into Granby, 20–21; in copper industry, 74; Granby director, 79
Nichols Chemical Company, New York, 16, 20
Nine Mile powersite: funds for, 63; construction of dam, 63–65
North Coast Railroad, 67
Northern Pacific Railroad: balks Blackwell, 54; service to Palouse area, 56–57; shares in S&IE, 69
Northwestern and Pacific Hypotheekbank: organized, 26; foreclosures, 29; donates parkland, 38

Old Ironsides mine, B.C., 5–6; report on ores, 8; company organized, 10
Olmsted, John C.: opinion of Rockwood, 48; opinion of Lincoln Heights, 51; on value of S&IE stock, 92
Olmsted Brothers: plan for Spokane, 39–40; design Rockwood area, 47; design Lincoln Heights area, 50; dun David Brown, 53; and Waikiki, 89, 90; parks plan of, 90

INDEX

Paine, Waldo G., 57, 61
Parks, Spokane: development, 33–34; Manito, 38; Audubon, 43–44; Cannon Hill, 44, 48–49; commission for, 46; bond issue for, 90
Peabody, Houghteling and Company, Chicago, 56
Phoenix, B.C.: description, 11–12, 14; miners' union, 14; ore traffic, 17; rail lines to, 77; abandoned, 86–87
Pope, Rufus H., 4
Provident Loan and Trust, 35

Railway Land and Improvement Company, 57
Recreation Park, Spokane, 42
Republic, Wash., mining district, 16
Republic & Kettle Valley Railroad, 16
Riblet, Byron C., 13
Richards, Henry, 43–44, 52
Ristine, George W., 56
Robinson, William H., 18, 77, 79
Rockwood district, Spokane, 47–48, 52, 53, 113n26, 114n30
Rodgers, M. K., 83
Rollins, E. H. and Sons, 56; sells S&IE bonds, 62–63; acquires S&IE, 72
Rossland, B.C., mining district, 8–9
Rutter, R. L., 90, 99–100

Sanderson and Porter engineering firm: builds Nine Mile dam, 65
Seven Troughs Reorganized Mining Company, Nevada, 99
Shaughnessy, Thomas G.: pushes Canadian Pacific to Boundary, 9; and James J. Hill, 15, 76, 79; Republic mines contract, 16; rejects second Boundary smelter, 19–20; opinion of Crow's Nest Pass Coal management, 75–76; promotes Corbin's Spokane International Railroad, 79–80; on returns from B.C. investment, 81
Sherwood, John D.: as agent for Adams Real Estate Trust, 40; develops Audubon, 43–44; on northwest Spokane, 47–48

Shuff, Carl A., 53, 73
Smith, C. A., 90, 93
Spokane, Columbia & Western Railroad, 117n16
Spokane, Portland, & Seattle Railroad, 71
Spokane, Wash.: description of, in 1888, 22, 24–26; growth of, 27–28, 32, 44–45; water system, 30–31, 46, 50; society, 37; charter, 46; overbuilt, 97; lot sizes, 109n14
Spokane & Eastern Railway & Power Company, 73
Spokane & Inland Empire Railroad: organization of predecessor lines, 55–60; town subsidies for, 57; loans to, 61, 66, 112n16; changes name, 61; stockholders, officers, 61; "preferred rights," 61, 118n20; construction, 63, 65, 66; buys Steptoe Butte, 63; power and sources, 63–65, 117n13; earnings, 66, 67–68; flooding, 66; service to patrons, 67; wreck 1909, 68–69; sells to Hill, 69; *Mining Truth* editorial on, 70; as Spokane, Portland & Seattle Rr. subsidiary, 71–72; goes to receiver, 72; last trains, 73
Spokane & Inland Railway. See Spokane & Inland Empire railroad
Spokane City Club: Graves's sale of, 89, 124n4
Spokane Country Club: original links, 38; Little Spokane site, 95, 111n6
Spokane Falls & Northern Railroad, 6, 32; and Boundary, 9, 15; sold to Great Northern, 106n17
Spokane International Railroad, 68; construction, 79–80. *See also* Canadian Pacific Railway; Corbin, Daniel C.; Shaughnessy, Thomas G.
Spokane Southern Traction Company, 41
Spokane Terminal Company, 55, 73
Spokane Traction Company: organized, 35–36, 111n2; franchises, 36–37, 41; lines to new areas, 51;

INDEX

Spokane Traction Company (*continued*)
Graves loses company, 51; earnings, 52; loan to, 55
Spokane-Washington Improvement Company: organized, 37–38, 111*n*6; develops Manito area, 38–39
Spokesman (Spokane): comments on Cedar bridge, 28–29
Spokesman-Review (Spokane): on parks, 33; on street railway competition, 36, 41; on S&IE wreck, 68; on Hill in S&IE, 69; on Graves's withdrawal from S&IE, 70
Stanton, John, 74–75, 79
Streetcar lines: in Spokane, 27–28; Montrose line, 35; Spokane Traction organized, 35–36; expanding routes, 41–44; to Lincoln Heights district, 50; falling patronage, 52; consolidation of routes, 52–53
Sussman, Otto: on Granby prospects, 74; on Granby reserves, 85
Sweeny, Charles, 30, 32
Sylvester, F. M., 85, 86

Title Guarantee and Trust Company, New York, 67
Towne, Mary Alice Hardin. *See* Mary Alice Graves
Traders National Bank (Spokane): loans to Graves, 55
Trail, B.C., smelter. *See* Canadian Pacific Railway
Tupper, Sir Charles, 4
Turner, George, 79, 99
Twohy, Denis D., 57

Valleyford, Wash., 57, 63
Van Valkenburg, Herman A., 26
Victoria, Vancouver & Eastern Railway & Navigation Company, 15; reaches Grand Forks, 77; B.C. compact with, 105*n*14. *See also* Hill, James Jerome

Waikiki: plans for, 89, 91–92; model farm, 96; bankers' appraisal, 100; Graveses sell, 101, 127*n*33
Warren, Dr. Frank F., 95, 102
Washington Water Power Company: and Graves's streetcar lines, 36–37, 43, 52; donates parkland, 38; on streetcar extensions, 41; increases stock, 42; rejects Graves's overture, 43; effect of competition on, 44; Graves proposes merger with, 63; buys remnants of S&IE, 73
Water systems, Spokane, 46, 50, 110*n*22
Weeks, Benjamin, 59, 63
Western Federation of Miners, 83
Western Miner: comment on Granby, 87
Western Trust and Investment Company, 50
White, Aubrey Lee, 4, 18, 74, 92, 93, 98; sells Graves's stock, moves to New York, 12; promotes parks, 39, 46, 88, 90; on Graves's real estate methods, 47; president of Hayden Lake Improvement Company, 60; joins S&IE board, 63; buys Graves's house, 90; short of money, 90–91; moves to Montvale, 97
White, William A., 63
White City, Spokane, 42
Whitney, Payne, 79, 90
Whitworth College, 93–95
Williams, William Yolen: description, 4; Granby manager, 11; removed as manager, 77; finds new mines, 83
Wooster, George W., 18

Zapata Corporation, 87